Gate

Jay and Meridel Rawlings

Jerusalem Israel
1985

New Wine Press
P.O. Box 17
Chichester
England

International Vistas
P.O. Box 8232
Jerusalem 91081
Israel

ISBN 0 947852 12 3

Printed in Great Britain by Anchor Brendon Ltd, Tiptree, Colchester, Essex.

Contents

Acknowledgements

We would like to say "thank you" to the many people who have worked so hard to make this book a reality. Special appreciation goes to Julia Martin and Florine Foerster who have laboured long hours in typing and retyping the several drafts. Thanks, also, to their understanding husbands and families.

We would also like to gratefully acknowledge our editor and co-publisher, Ed Harding, in England. He made numerous timely and helpful suggestions during the book's gestation period.

Most of all, we would like to thank the Jewish men and women that we met particularly those in the U.S.S.R. who were willing to speak to us from their hearts in spite of the ever present threat of the KGB.

Finally, we give praise and thanks to the God of Israel for His guidance, encouragement and inspiration.

Foreword

by Martin Gilbert

Every effort to help those Soviet Jews who wish to do so to leave the Soviet Union for Israel is to be welcomed. So too is every forum in which those Soviet Jews who wish to do so may be allowed to put forward their own thoughts and appeals.

Twenty years ago, Soviet Jews were known as the Jews of silence. Today, with great courage, they dare to contact us, to pass on to us their messages, their fears, the facts of their current plight, and above all, continually, to demand the right of an exit visa.

The courage of these people in speaking to us demands that we try to reciprocate with the clearest possible advocacy of their situation.

Today more than twelve per cent of the world's Jews live in the Soviet Union. Numbering at least two million, they are scattered in several hundred localities, only a few of which are accessible to the Western visitor. Cut off from any real practice of their religious beliefs, customs, festivals and teachings, the Jews of the Soviet Union are also a national group. They have the word "Jew" inscribed in the nationality section of their internal passport document.

Soviet Jews are a national group, however, cut

off from their Jewish national home, the State of Israel, even though the Soviet Union, together with the United States, voted in favour of a Jewish State in November 1947 at the United Nations, and recognized Israel's Independence at the moment of statehood in May 1948.

Between 1970 and 1979, a period of detente, the Soviet Union allowed more than a quarter of a million Jews to leave the Soviet Union. This was a substantial and remarkable exodus. But for the last five years the doors of exit have been effectively shut.

More than twelve thousand Jews are now living 'in refusal', as it is called. They are the 'refuseniks' who look to us for help, appealing to us not only as a question of individual need, but in search of a mechanism, an international mechanism, whereby all who wish to leave can be released. For these twelve thousand, and for as many as 360,000 who have indicated that they would like to be able to leave, their need today is that they should become an integral part of the Soviet-American negotiation process, and of the actual decisions which lie in front of us in the international arena.

There are more than twenty-five Jews in prison, labour camp or exile today for their part in assisting the process of Jewish national awakening in the Soviet Union, for seeking to teach a modicum of Jewish history, the Hebrew language, and the Jewish religious heritage. Yosef Begun, who is now 52 years old, must remain a prisoner until he is 63 for his part in seeking to impart the rudiments of Jewish teaching.

In labour camp today, Anatoly Shcharansky enters his seventh year as a prisoner for demanding the right to leave and live as a Jew in Israel.

Shcharansky, like his fellow Jewish activists, never sought to change the Soviet Union; they understood that its structures could not be changed. His only wish, since 1971, was to leave the Soviet Union. In labour camp today, Shcharansky draws solace from his knowledge of the Psalms, and in the monthly letters which he is only allowed to write as a result of a health-crippling hunger strike, he discusses the theological and spiritual meaning and relevance of each Psalm, letter by letter.

Ten years ago, any Jew who was released from prison, received his exit visa and left the Soviet Union. Since 1980 not a single released prisoner has been allowed to leave. Ida Nudel, who is now 54 years old, is refused permission to join her only sister who lives in Israel, despite the fact that she has long ago served her term for having had the audacity to raise a little banner on her apartment balcony: "Give me my visa for Israel". Evgeny Lein, another released prisoner, is not only refused permission to leave, but was recently beaten up in the street for daring to continue his effort on behalf of fellow Jews.

The Jews of Russia ask the Jews in the West if it is not possible, when devising a mechanism in which detente and human rights are linked, whereby the prisoners, and the former prisoners, might be given some priority for consideration of exit visas.

The question is not merely how to help individuals, painful though their plight may be. It is how to proceed so that the quarter of a million exit visas granted to Soviet Jews between 1970 and

1979 may once again become a reality, a renewed norm.

The Jews of Russia urge us to put forward a series of arguments at the highest level of international diplomacy. One such argument is to insist that the Soviet Union honour its signature of the Helsinki Accords of 1975. These accords established on a foundation of international agreement the right of any person to leave any country 'including his own' and to go to any country.

A second argument which Soviet Jews expect us to urge on their behalf is the right of divided families to be re-united. This too is an integral part of the Helsinki Accords, so solemnly signed by Moscow as well as by Washington. If these agreements are to be flouted, can new agreements on arms control or trade have any more binding force?

A third argument put forward by Soviet Jews, for us to press on their behalf, is one which would benefit every Soviet Jew who has asked to leave Russia for Israel. This is the argument that what is at issue is not emigration, but repatriation: the right of Jews anywhere in the world to be repatriated to the Jewish State, just as Armenians living in Turkey or the United States may, under Soviet rules, be repatriated to Soviet Armenia.

There is a fourth argument which many Soviet Jews would like to see given serious consideration in the diplomatic arena. This concerns the rights of nearly 900 Jews, and their number is rising every week, who have requested, and received, Israeli citizenship. These 900 wish to be considered as Israeli citizens living overseas, for whom the State of Israel, or its representatives such as the Dutch Embassy in Moscow, can urge their swiftest possible transfer to the land for which they possess a Nationality Certificate. This land, Israel, is after all a member state of the United Nations, a state with dual nationality agreements with several other states, and a state willing to receive them at any time.

Those Soviet Jews who ask for them are convinced that if we in the West go about it in the right way, such certificates (many of the most recent signed by the Israeli prime minister himself while he was acting minister of the interior) could be a means, within the framework of some international negotiation, of securing them an exit visa. Cannot we parallel their courage in acquiring these certificates by our ingenuity in working out ways whereby these treasured documents will serve as a passport to Israel, the state which has issued them?

Nine of today's Prisoners of Zion hold Israeli citizenship; they possess the precious Nationality Certificate issued from Jerusalem. Could not the International Red Cross be mobilized on their behalf? Or the International Court at the Hague?

Soviet Jews believe that each of the above arguments could be a part of bilateral negotiations between the Soviet Union and any Western state which is concerned with the plight of Soviet Jewry. In the coming year of intense East-West negotiations, and as plans are being made for President Reagan to meet Chairman Gorbachev, it is surely up to us to ensure that the future of those tens of thousands of Soviet Jews who wish to live in Israel is not only kept on the agenda of the negotiations, but is made an integral part of any agreement. Such is the message from Moscow today.

Soviet Jews anticipate that the years 1985 and 1986 may see an intensification of official Soviet pressure on the Jewish activists. They also anticipate that the same two years may see considerable progress in the sphere of East-West dialogue. But they know that such dialogue, as it leads, they trust, to detente, cannot help them unaided. Help can only come, they feel, if Jews in the West maintain the pressure on their own governments to ensure that Soviet Jews are part of the future bargaining process. Only then will exit visas and peaceful co-exitstence go hand-in-hand.

Martin Gilbert

Preface

'I will break in pieces the gates of brass, and cut apart the bars of iron.'
Jeremiah 16:14-15

These words, spoken by the Lord to King Cyrus, signalled the liberation of the Jews from Babylonian captivity. Jewish history, it seems, does repeat itself. Cyrus, a gentile ruler hundreds of years after Pharaoh, listened to God and thereby participated in the fulfillment of Bible prophecy. Cyrus willingly released the Jews to their prophetic call, while Pharaoh of Egypt was forced by the hand of God to release the captives in the midst of national disaster.

Today the world is divided into two camps when it comes to Israel and the Jews: those who will encourage them along their prophetic pathway and those who will hinder and prevent them from entering into their God-given position in history. Secular and religious indifference toward the Jews is regarded in the same light by God who spoke these words to Abraham:

'And I will establish my covenant between me and thee and thy seed after thee in their generations for an EVERLASTING COVENANT, to be a God unto thee, and to thy seed after thee.

And I will give unto thee, and thy seed after thee, the land wherein thou art a stranger, all the land of Canaan, for an EVERLASTING POSSESSION; and I will be their God.'

Genesis 17:7-8

The Jews are inseparable from the land of promise because of the covenants of God. Pharaoh had to let the Jews go because of the covenant or contract of the Lord. The release of the Jews from Egyptian bondage is remembered and celebrated each year in the observance of Passover when Jewish families the world over look back to their corporate preservation. Each family selects their youngest member and he or she asks the question, "Why is this night different from any other?" Of course the answer comes back in the form of gratefulness to the Lord for their release from Egyptian slavery.

Did you know that the scriptures point forward to a time when this, the most time-honoured annual celebration of world Jewry, will be eclipsed? Listen to the words of Jeremiah, the great prophet:

' "However the days are coming," declares the Lord, "when men will no longer say, 'As surely as the Lord lives, who brought the Israelites up out of Egypt,' but they will say, 'As surely as the Lord lives, who brought the Israelites up out of the land of the north and out of all the countries where he had banished them.' For I will restore them to the land I gave

to their forefathers.'
Jeremiah 16:14-15

This scripture has never been fulfilled in previous migrations of the Jewish people. Any Bible atlas reveals that the northern dispersion of the Jews involved the areas of Georgia, the Crimea, Turkey, Southern Russia and even into Western Russia and Poland. The city of Moscow is directly north of Jerusalem. Some three million Jews have made the "land of the north" their home for centuries. During the last one hundred years a slow but distinct migration of this population has occurred. The first waves of Russian "aliyah", meaning "crossing over" or "going up" to Israel occurred in the 1880's and brought thousands of young Russian Jews to the Promised Land then known as Palestine, while others went elsewhere to find their fortunes. In the spring of 1917 the Russian revolution birthed by the writings of Karl Marx and administered by the skill of Vladimir Lenin spelled doom for the Russian Jewish community. By October 1917 the revolution had developed into brutality and terror for the Jews.

Slowly but surely the will of the Soviet system was turned against the Jews or "Zionists" as they later became known for their desire to emigrate to Israel. Waves of immigration started to flow from Russia for the next fifty years, in spite of enormous obstacles and difficulties. Also, we must remember that most of the founding fathers of the State of Israel came from Russia. Unquestionably the population of the Palestine was infused with new vigour by the Russian emigration of 1880 to 1930. The same is true today.

It is estimated that during the Stalin era some

twenty to sixty million people died in the Soviet Union. Fear and terror gripped the minds of the populace. The Jews, however, were being awakened to their prophetic place and their call to "cross over" to Israel began to arise in their hearts. This pull homeward and upward was stronger than the downward one of death and destruction, perpetrated by the Soviet regime. Slowly the demand on the Jewish conscience to escape this cauldron of horror and sin has been growing and now directly confronts the enormous Soviet system.

Communism is doomed to fail because it works contrary to the principles of God. It subjugates the will of the people to the will of the State. This is in direct opposition to the divine principle which never has and never will make robots of men. The free enterprise economic system, with all its weaknesses, is still more closely aligned to God's principles than the Communist socialist system which removes the initiative of the individual. The free-will choice of Russian Jews to go to Israel will eventually overrule the Soviet system.

The heartbeat of freedom has continued to burn in the breast of the Jews in difficult captivities throughout their history. The events taking place in Israel have been like a shofar[1] call to the souls of Jews who will respond the world over. The psalmist David understood this principle when he wrote:

'You will arise and have compassion on Zion, for it is time to show favour to her; the appointed time has come.

For her stones are dear to your servants; her very dust moves them to pity. The nations will

1 *Ram's horn trumpet*

fear the name of the Lord, all the kings of the earth will revere your glory.

For the Lord will rebuild Zion and appear in his glory.

He will respond to the prayer of the destitute; he will not despise their plea.

Let this be written for a future generation[1], that a people not yet created may praise the Lord:

"The Lord looked down from his sanctuary on high, from heaven he viewed the earth, to hear the groans of the prisoners and release those condemned to death."

So the name of the Lord will be declared in Zion and his praise in Jerusalem.'

Psalm 102:13-21

Today with five million prisoners in the USSR, and many condemned to death, the characteristic of the God of Israel that gives us the courage is that He always keep His word and will respond to those who believe it and have faith. The Jews will come out of Russia simply because God's word declares that they will. There is a battle to be won – a battle of faith. This book portrays the contestants in this battle.

[1] *In Hebrew: "The Last Generation"*

1

The Heart

"You dirty zhid![1] You need to die!" With these words ringing in his ears, thirteen-year-old Carmi Elbert fell to the ground as he was being struck on the head and back with an iron bar and kicked repeated by his classmates.

"You and your parents are enemies of the Soviet State; we'll teach you a lesson you'll never forget!" As he slipped into unconsciousness blood oozed from his ears and nose. Suffering severe internal injuries, Carmi faintly remembered the KGB Colonel's words spoken to his father, "You will NOT be present at your son's Bar Mitzvah!"

Almost unconscious, Carmi's mind registered that this was the day of his Bar Mitzvah and sadly recalled that his father was now in prison. Their love for Israel had seemed so clean, so real. He often recalled the day seven years before when his father, Lev, came home and began whispering to his mother Inna. They had started to think about applying to leave Russia for Israel. This type of thinking was dangerous for Russian Jews, and needed to be approached with the utmost caution.

[1] *'zhid' – Russian derogatory slang for Jew.*

Lev's job as a chemical engineer and Inna's as a cardiologist would be in danger if the authorities knew of their hope and aspirations as a family to go to their ancient homeland, Israel.

Day by day the longing grew in Lev's heart for the land of the Bible, the land of his forefathers. At birth his father and mother had named him Lev, which in Hebrew means 'heart'. His life had reflected a largeness of heart and love for his God, family, ancient homeland and fellow Jews. Carmi remembered the long hours his father spent during the Russian winter toiling over the scriptures and teaching himself how to read, write and speak in the 'tongue of the prophets' Hebrew. The ancient words of Jeremiah and Isaiah came alive to Lev and he began to share his excitement in biblical discovery with his family. Soon Carmi's uncle, Michael, began to study with his father and they shared their new love of the Torah together. The desire to leave for Israel spread to other family members and close friends. Finally, the came to apply for an 'exit' visa to Israel. The Elberts decided to apply together, so Carmi's uncle Alexander, Mrs Misruchin on his mother's side, a doctor of psychiatry, Grandma and Grandpa Haim Elbert and Uncle Michael all applied to go to Israel. That was when everything began to change.

Immediately they were placed under suspicion and Lev was fired from his job. Inna was not fired immediately as she was needed in the community. She worked as the cardiologist in charge of an ambulance team that would respond to emergency and cardiac calls. Her job was to resuscitate those who had had cardiac arrests. The only job Lev could get was that of an artist's model. It was degrading for a practising Jew, but he had no choice. Several months later Inna was also fired.

The experiences of the Elbert family are typical for Jews in the Soviet Union who apply to leave for Israel. In order to obtain an exit visa one needs a 'karacteristika' or reference from one's place of work. As soon as this document is requested one is fired. To be unemployed in the Soviet Union is tantamount to villainy. One who has no job becomes a 'hooligan or parasite' on Soviet society. Lev Elbert and his family were now 'enemies of the people'.

Carmi lay crumpled on the still-frozen ground, smeared by blood, unable to move without excruciating pain, for what seemed an eternity. Finally he heard the cries of his mother who, believing he was dead, was near hysteria.

Slowly she and Grandpa Haim gathered him gently in their arms and carried him through the evening darkness to their second-floor apartment. This was the day of Carmi's thirteenth birthday, his Bar Mitzvah, which in the Jewish tradition is the day when a boy becomes a man. Carmi had become a man.

His eyes were swollen nearly shut, his eyesight severely damaged. Blood appeared in his urine, indicative of the severity of the kicks he received to his kidneys. Later, x-rays showed that one kidney and his spleen had been kicked out of place. Dr. Inna nursed her son at home the best she could, afraid to take him to the hospital. She too had been fired from her position as cardiologist due to 'excessive absences' when she was fasting ten and thirty-seven days respectively for the release of her husband Lev, who was in prison on trumped-up charges.

Unfortunately Carmi did not know it, but that very day many thirteen-year-olds the world over were celebrating twin Bar Mitzvahs with him. Jewish boys were celebrating in Australia, England, USA, Canada and South Africa in Bar Mitzvahs where Carmi Elbert was remembered and honoured. This is the miracle of Jewish connectedness which preserves their faith. Photographs that we took of Carmi when we visited his home months earlier were sent around the world by Ruth Barron, the director of the Israel Public Committee on Soviet Jewry. The gathering of these photographs and how we met the Elbert family personally in Kiev is one of the reasons for this book and the film, 'Gates of Brass'.

Background

It was in September 1980 that the International Christian Embassy was formed in Jerusalem. Meridel and I had the privilege of being among the initiators of this important, timely work which has mushroomed in five years as one of the fastest-growing organizations in the world. Its purpose and function is two-fold: to show the Jewish people that they have friends worldwide who are working for their good according to Holy Scripture, and secondly to educate the Christian Community worldwide about the scriptural basis of this support for Israel. One of the early functions of the ICEJ was to establish a Soviet Jewry desk and to mobilize worldwide Christian support on behalf of the 'refuseniks', those Jews denied exit visas.

It was September 1982, when Meridel and I, with hundreds of other Christians, were busy preparing for the annual Christian Celebration during the Feast of Tabernacles in Jerusalem. We were in the largest conference centre in the city, the Binyanae Ha Oma, or The Building of the People, when two ladies from Holland came up on the platform and stopped all the activity with this question. "Have you heard what is happening to the famous Russian Jewish refusenik, Anatoly Shcharansky?" Sheepishly we had to admit we did not know the latest news. They explained that he was in the midst of a hunger strike, in very critical physical condition. Rumours had it that the Russians were force-feeding him in his jail cell. He was fasting because he had been denied the right to send or receive letters. Even this was a violation of the laws of the Soviet penal system. Anatoly Shcharansky had been put into jail as a 'traitor' to the Soviet Union for having had contact with foreign journalists and tourists. Now, seven years later and halfway through his sentence, his life was hanging in the balance.

Immediately work was stopped for prayer. We must remember Anatoly and his wife Avital who has tirelessly travelled the globe seeking support for his release from government leaders and free citizens alike, worldwide. Prayer was directed to the Lord requesting world leaders, Presidents and Premiers of European and Western powers to bring pressure to bear on the Soviets to adhere to the UN Charter of Human Rights and the Helsinki Accord. Suddenly, as if wind came from heaven, the Lord spoke in a prophetic word through Meridel.

"Why do you look to the East, or to the West, the North or South? Does not my word say that deliverance will come from Zion? Blow the trumpet in Zion, sound the alarm, call an assembly of the peoples. Set your face against the North; let your foreheads be as brass. From here a small company will go unto the North country and speak a word of release to my people."

Silence filled that great auditorium as Israeli workers, technicians and Christians alike sensed the weight of the word that had come 'from on high'. The divine challenge and call had been issued. Who would respond? Later that day Meridel and I discussed the prophecy and we agreed that if we could do anything as a couple we would make ourselves available, even if it meant a return visit to the USSR.

The next day we were all extremely busy with the opening of the Feast. Four thousand people from forty-one nations had come up to Jerusalem. In spite of these activities, in a quiet moment just before one of the seminars on Soviet Jewry, Meridel asked the Lord . . . "When?" The answer came back immediately . . . "Pesach!" Hebrew for Passover.

We received our sealed orders and tucked this knowledge away with grateful hearts. We began to prepare to go to the USSR for Passover which included believing for the necessary finances, visas, passports and contacts. Passports were a major consideration as ours had been issued through the Canadian Embassy in Tel Aviv. The Israeli stamps in our passports could veto the entire trip, but we continued to proceed with our plans.

By late January 1983 we received a phone call from our friend, Rev. Clyde Williamson, assistant pastor at Queensway Cathedral, one of Canada's most vibrant churches. Clyde mentioned that senior Pastor Ralph Rutledge had called the church to a forty day fast which began on January 1st, 1983. The church was three weeks into this fast when a powerful message was given by Clyde who prophesied that this congregation and the church, worldwide, was called to believe for revival, to bless Israel and help the Soviet Jews get back to Israel. Everyone was challenged to an 'Esther Fast' of three days without food or drink on April 1st, 2nd and 3rd, 1983.

These were the same dates that I had just arranged to be in Moscow with Meridel and our 12-year-old son, Chris. We knew that this was not just a coincidence and that our schedule was divinely arranged. The Lord then spoke to Meridel and myself to complete the Esther fast before going into the Soviet Union. While in Russia we would represent those who were fasting worldwide.

Simultaneously the Russian Jews living in Jerusalem were painfully aware of the severe conditions faced by their friends and family in the USSR. Their statement to the 2000 delegates at the 3rd Brussels World Conference on Soviet Jewry, March 15th to 17th in Jerusalem was as follows:

To: Delegates of the Third World Conference on Soviet Jewry:
Honoured ladies and gentlemen:

" . . . We feel that the situation of Soviet Jews is such that their physical existence is under threat.

We are convinced that the resolutions of our conference should be based on an understanding of this threat.

Thirty years ago, only a miracle saved Soviet Jews. Stalin's death saved them from mass deportation to Siberia, a fate suffered by other minorities, which led to the deaths of hundreds of thousands of people. The country was behind an iron curtain and of these committed and planned crimes, the world found out only much later. Only the realization of this reality will give our actions the sense of urgency capable of preventing a tragic course of events.

Have we the right to hope only for a miracle?"

Signed by Russian Jews now resident in Israel.

Dr. Lev Utevsky, a research scientist and recent arrival from Leningrad summed up his presentation at the Brussels conference with this statement: "If we shall not succeed in rescuing these Jewish men and women, fighting in the USSR for Jewish souls . . . I personally shall not be able to read, without deep pangs of conscience, the following words of our Bible, the words with which our greatest king ordered the betrayal of his faithful warrior.

'Set Uriah in the forefront of the hardest fighting and then draw back from him, that he may be struck down and die.'

2 Samuel 11:15

At the same time, a worldwide campaign of free Soviet Jews and Christians was initiated by the International Christian Embassy in Jerusalem on March 16th 1983. This was called the 'Mordecai Outcry' demonstration. Hundreds of Christians gathered on the Knesset grounds in Jerusalem to express solidarity with Israel in this struggle. Upon hearing of these actions, the Soviet Jewry

Committee of the Knesset was not only surprised but delighted. They had long wanted to organize similar worldwide protests but lacked the time and manpower needed.

Demonstrations similar to the Jerusalem 'Mordecai Outcry' were successfully staged outside Soviet Embassies in Copenhagen, Stockholm, London, Dublin, Paris, Washington D.C., Ottawa and Canberra. While in the Hague, 3,000 people gathered in front of the Soviet Embassy to support Soviet Jewry. Further actions were also held in Switzerland, Norway, Germany and New Zealand.

At the same time in Washington the Congressional records report that in March, 1983, Congressman Siljander from Michigan, Congressman Smith from New Jersey and Senator Boren of Oklahoma, a bipartisan group of Republicans and Democrats on both sides of Capitol Hill, announced the beginning of a week called the 'Mordecai Outcry Week'. They said:

'The International Christian Embassy in Jerusalem has announced that this is a major project of the Christian community throughout the world. As we all know, Mordecai cried for release of the Jews when he uncovered a plot to destroy them, and he appealed to Queen Esther, his niece, to go to the King to speak out on behalf of those who were to be oppressed.

'Today we in the Congress, modern-day Mordecais, so to speak, raise our voices in crying out to the world to please come to the rescue of Anatoly Shcharansky and the beleaguered Russian Jews. Anatoly is one of the giant dissidents and prisoners of conscience in the Soviet Union. I would like to thank my Congressmen and Senator friends and identify myself in a statement of solidarity that Jewish and Christian, Democrats and Republicans and folks all over the world, are lending their voices to this very worthwhile effort. It is absolutely imperative that the USSR hear our voices, hear our cries, hear the cries of people in this country and throughout the world who speak LET MY PEOPLE GO, Shcharansky, Nudel, Slepak and many others behind the iron wall who need us to speak for them.'

Agents to the North Country

On March 20, 1983, while the International Christian Embassy was demonstrating for the release of the Soviet Jews at the Knesset[1] in Jerusalem, we were being whisked by a 'sheroot' or Israeli taxi through the Plains of Esdralon towards Ben Gurion airport. Our destination was the USSR.

The needed funds came from concerned Christians all over Israel, Europe, Canada and the USA which helped purchase the necessary air tickets and Intourist vouchers for travel in the USSR.

We carried messages from former refuseniks now living in Israel, and from representatives of the North American committees for the freedom of Soviet Jews. We had shared the plans of our adventure with Naomi Teasdale at Jerusalem's city hall. In response, Mayor Teddy Kollek gave us two dozen golden lapel buttons of the 'Lion of the Tribe of Judah' symbol of Jerusalem, normally reserved as a gift for special guests to the city. These pins

[1] *Hebrew equivalent of Congress of Parliament in Israel*

were to be given with the mayor's personal greetings to the refuseniks we would meet. The pins symbolize the ancient Jewish hope expressed every Passover: 'Next Year In Jerusalem'. We also carried greetings from the International Christian Embassy, and represented Queensway Cathedral in Toronto who initiated the call to thousands of dedicated Christians around the world who would be entering into the Esther fast.

Most westerners visiting the USSR for the first, second and even third time, encounter a devastating 'culture shock'. One is greeted with silence, unsmiling faces and the atmosphere of tension and suspicion. 'Guilty until proven innocent' seems to be the rule there, frustratingly illustrated by standing for two hours, waiting to be processed through passport control. There is no concept of the 'customer is right' and the most simple request becomes a nightmare. We understood that we were dealing with a system aimed at producing intimidation and fear, and our hearts went out to all Soviet people.

Kiev

Kiev, capital of the Ukraine, is known as the mother of Russian towns. It was 1.30 a.m. when we arrived. As our bus approached the city, search lights lit up the dark night illuminating a massive one hundred and two metre high white statue of 'Mother Russia'. She commanded attention situated on a cliff high above the Dniper River. We derived no sense of maternal comfort or warmth from this monstrous and muscular portrayal of

Motherhood. Upon arrival at the hotel, in spite of our weariness, we were aware of the many grim-faced men standing in the lobby watching who came in and went out. Were they KGB agents?

From his bed Chris easily picked out the microphones by following the ceiling wires with his gaze. We fell into an exhausted sleep to be awakened at 3.30 a.m. by the telephone. "Hello. Hello?" The only response was a deliberate 'click'. The anonymous caller hung up.

By mid-morning we had recovered from jet lag and were being taxied about this historic city of trees and parks. Weak spring sunshine gave 1,500-year-old Kiev a very tired and worn appearance. Our guide pointed out that the apostle Andrew arrived in Kiev in the first century B.C. to preach to the wild tribe people. In 988 Prince Vladimir officially adopted Christianity. He enlarged and fortified his city strategically located on the banks of the mighty 2,285 kilometre-long Dniper River. This strategic body of water flows from the steppes of Russia out to the Black Sea in the south.

Kiev's history is one of intrigue, bloody battles and conquest. Time was etched upon the buildings. Golden domes towering high above the churches carried us back over the centuries. Our guide mentioned that in spite of the fact that only 8% of the population attend church, the city boasts many great cathedrals such as the Sofia Cathedral built in 1037, Vladimer's Cathedral and other famous monasteries. Today these churches house museums in which the Soviets have carefully and cleverly interspersed biblical truths with Egyptology, Greek mythology and Soviet propaganda. Christianity is cunningly displayed as stemming from witchcraft and sorcery. Recent Soviet history is carefully traced to the degeneration of the rich Russian Orthodox priesthood depicted as Nazi collaborators. The priests are portrayed as being directly responsible for the deaths of 20 million Russians in World War Two. Large murals suggest that the responsibility for centuries of serfdom and depression lie on the Church's doorstep, while communism is presented as the true saviour of mankind, bringing bread to the hungry, clothes to the naked, comfort, succour and dignity to the poor masses. The conclusion ... communism alone has delivered her peoples who for centuries were the pawn of an evil church system!

Because it was the Easter season, or in modern Soviet terminology, 'the spring break' the museums were jammed with Soviet people who had no way of discerning fact from fiction. All in all, it was a depressing and sobering experience. As much as we enjoyed touring, our prime purpose for visiting Kiev at this time had not been realised.

An air of heaviness hung over the city and one couldn't help but wonder if history would repeat itself. During World War Two, when the Nazis invaded Kiev, the first act of establishing their supremacy was to demand the hanging of local Jews. On that unforgettable day three thousand were hung on the main street of this city. How could the Nazis find them so quickly? Simple ... the local inhabitants turned them in. Today a reign of KGB terror continues against specific Jews there. Perhaps their plan is to single them out as examples for other 'refuseniks' in the U.S.S.R. We sensed that time was of the essence for the evening of our first day was 'Erev Pessach' or the first evening of Passover. We were hoping to make contact with the Elbert family, leaders in the Jewish Community.

Many long hours were spent looking for our friends. To avoid KGB bugging it meant finding public telephones in obscure places to make initial contact before travelling to an unknown address. Searching out a hidden and despised people is a hair-raising past-time and we never got used to it. Our first attempts were unsuccessful. We searched out the correct street in upper Kiev, sensing how conspicuous we were in Western dress. We quickly walked to the apartment of Michael Elbert and climbed the creaking, dingy stairway to his door. Seeing the mezzuah[1], I knew we had found the correct apartment. Momentary joy flooded our hearts but soon dissipated when no-one answered our knock. In response the door to the adjacent apartment opened and a young girl looked up. Her mouth fell open with shock and she closed the door immediately. We were apprehensive and left for fear that she would suspect something and alert the local informer of the KGB. Every apartment house has one.

Sensing an urgency to make contact with this family, two hours later we again went to Michael's home. Still no-one answered the door. We were cautioned not to bring Lev's address as he was under continual surveillance. We were stuck, it seemed, and had no way of contacting him other than through Michael. We composed the following note in Hebrew:

[1] *A mezzuah is a small cylindrical container created specifically to hold Scriptures (Deuteronomy, chapter 6:9) which is obediently tacked to the doorposts of Jewish homes.*

"Greetings from your family in Israel. Meet us tomorrow at 4 p.m. in the zoo by the bears."

I folded it very carefully and slipped it into the crack of the door. We left unnoticed.

By this time it was 5 p.m. and the setting of the sun would bring in Passover. We made a quick decision and decided to take the taxi down to Lower Kiev where the only synagogue in this city of several million people was situated. I had memorised the location. We disembarked from our vehicle several blocks away and walked from there to the synagogue. Double doors, covered by peeling green paint, showed their years of neglect. They stood ajar and led into the courtyard. In previous visits to synagogues in many nations of the world, we have always been cordially greeted. Kiev was different. Small groups of elderly gentlemen eyed our approach but continued their discussions just as though we weren't visible. After some minutes of standing alone trying not to feel conspicuous, an elderly man came up to us and questioned unfeelingly, "Why have you come here?"

"We have come to celebrate Pesach, Hag Samach!"[1] I said, trying to sound at ease.

"Where are you from?" he enquired in English.

"Canada" I replied.

Just then a handsome man wearing a bright green kippa joined us, extended his hand in a very friendly manner and said, "Shalom, I'm Matthew."

The elderly man eyed us from a distance, came and interrupted our conversation. "Don't talk here. You'll get us all into trouble. Wait until you can speak in the street." Then it was time for the evening service to begin and we were led into the

[1] *'Hag Samach': A Hebrew greeting for happy holidays.*

faded pink stucco synagogue.

On the walls of the entrance hall we were careful to note many nicely framed 5x7 photographs of the Jews of Kiev celebrating their various holidays. Purim, Pessach, Shauvot Sinchat Torah and Hannukah. To the casual observer it appeared that there was great religious freedom for the Jews here. We knew much better.

Chris and I were escorted to the front pew and seated close to the 'bema' or place from which the scriptures are read. This way there was no chance that we could speak with any of the local congregation. Meridel made her way up the old wooden staircase to the women's balcony. The lights were turned on and the cantor began to sing. Erev Pesach had arrived. The immediate impression was that the synagogue was not used regularly. During the course of the service, I went outside in search of a washroom. To my amazement, the courtyard was filled with plainclothes KGB. Dressed in their dark suits, overcoats and hats, and some with dark glasses, they stood questioning the older men who had eyed us upon arrival. I quickly turned and walked away. At the close of the service, when we returned to the courtyard, not one agent was to be found. I was sure they had found us out before we had even begun our most important work.

The following day we waited impatiently, wondering if we would be able to meet the Elberts. Finally about 3 p.m. we made our way to the zoo. We weren't sure that the Elberts had even received the message or that if they had, they might disregard it as a KGB trick. Also, we didn't know what Lev and Michael looked like so it would be hard to identify them. Nevertheless at 4 p.m., while purchasing the tickets for the zoo, I saw the two brothers coming down the street.

As if by some supernatural radar, I knew them instantly and whispered to Meridel, "Don't look now but here they come." When they came into the zoo, I said in a stage whisper, "Come on, let's go right over to the bears." A few moments later, while watching the animals, Michael Elbert came up beside me and while we both looked straight ahead he whispered a Hebrew word that sounded like music to my ears . . . "Shalom".

Meanwhile Lev stood beside Meridel with Chris in the middle. They began to talk quietly. Gradually Michael, Lev and I started to walk together and to speak. My heart burned within when he began to tell me his story.

"In 1976 I applied for a visa to immigrate with Inna and Carmi to Israel. The application was refused on the grounds that I had served in the Russian Army and thus 'had been exposed to state secrets'. This is a common ploy used by the Soviet authorities to deny exit visas to 'refuseniks'. By January 1980 the Russian government lifted this security bar. It gave us new hope and by late 1981 Inna's mother and brother were granted visas and were living in Israel. However, in spite of this, Inna and I were repeatedly refused exit visas on the basis that we had 'insufficient kinship' in Israel. This was another Soviet trick violating the U.N. Charter of Human Rights, the Helsinki Accord and the Soviet Constitution guaranteeing 'rights for the reunification of families'.

Then the force of anti-semitism that has surfaced in the Soviet Union over the centuries really came against us. We were harassed, beaten and arrested on many occasions. One night the KGB were waiting for Inna when she came off duty at the hospital. In an isolated spot at the end of the bus line they beat her up and left her bleeding in the snow. In 1979 I was arrested and imprisoned for fifteen days on the false charge of 'petty hooliganism'. This internment was timed to prevent my participation in commemoration of the Babi Yar massacre[1]. While in jail and my whereabouts were unknown to my family, the police told my distraught relatives that they 'must look for me in a morgue'. As a result of this worry my father had a stroke and lost 50% of his eyesight. Michael, my brother, was also beaten by the KGB and had to disguise the bruises on his face when he went to visit father in the hospital to prevent a relapse."

As we strolled the footpaths at the zoo Lev went on with his story. "In September, 1980, there were KGB searches in Lev and Michael's apartments with confiscation of books in Hebrew and English and some old Russian books on Jewish history and Judaism." He continued, "'They then threatened me with a trial on a charge of spreading anti-Soviet propaganda. Then I was invited to the KGB headquarters and demanded that I stop the flow of letters and telegrams for my defence from London. This was a definite indication of the influence of letters from abroad," he pointed out.

In May 1981 an article appeared in the Kiev newspaper entitled 'Paskudnike' or 'Scoundrels' which claimed that "Lev Elbert sells tendentious

[1] "Babi Yar" *is the place just outside Kiev where nearly 100,000 Jews were massacred by the Nazis on September 29th 1941.*

information abroad, a crime for which some citizens of the U.S.S.R. received terms of many years".

In August 1981 Inna's mother was told by the KGB just before her emigration to Israel, "You will never see your daughter or grandson again." She still weeps over this statement. "Recently," Lev continued to explain, "Evgeny Barror, a long-term 'refusenik' and friend, was detained in the street. The KGB told him that his exit visa would be taken away if he refused to sign a testimony about my anti-Soviet activity and passing of inflammatory information abroad. Fortunately he refused. In spite of these terror tactics and threats he later received his exit visa and happily arrived in Israel. In late 1982 I was told by the Chief of the Kiev immigration office that 'refusal' to the Elbert family will continue an additional ten years."

"Just recently I had a visit from the KGB Colonel to try to intimidate me to stop any contacts with tourists and telephone conversations with foreigners. During our three-hour 'talk' the Colonel said, 'Some time ago we only had evidence to charge you on the basis of Article 190, which is slander against the Soviet Union, but now we have additional evidence so we can charge you on Article 70 which means you have participated in anti-Soviet activity, so we can imprison you for a long period, up to ten years. Your son will grow up while you are in a concentration camp. It will be impossible to help with his future education or even to attend his Bar Mitzvah.' "

We walked around the zoological gardens, pausing briefly to look at the various animals. The conversation revealed the cry of Lev's soul. I asked him, "What can we do for you?" His reply, "Please don't forget us. Go everywhere and make a noise for us. Tell people in the free world that by their silence they are condoning the genocide of my people."

I promised Lev and Michael that we would do our best to help them. The night began to close in around us as we left the zoo. In parting Lev asked us to come to visit his home the next day. Of course we were eager to continue our contact but I protested. "I don't want to jeopardize you and your family by our presence."

We knew that it would be dangerous for Soviet citizens to entertain foreigners. Lev threw back his head and laughed. "You will come for tea at 4 p.m. tomorrow. I want you to meet Inna and Carmi".

We returned to our hotel challenged by the courage and pluck of the Elbert brothers. Over dinner we dared not speak about our day's activities but neither could we put our friends out of our minds.

The following day we carefully made our way to Lev's home by public transport. We did our best not to draw attention to our movements. The April spring had not yielded to the Ukranian winter and a biting north wind gusted around as we left the bus. It roared off, leaving a cloud of diesel fumes. Feeling 'exposed' we searched the street in both directions and to our relief saw no tails or KGB agents. We found the Elbert apartment building and entered from the rear . . . they were fortunate as the building faced a valley of trees, albeit stripped bare by the icy Siberian winds. We quickly mounted the wooden stairs. I pressed the door bell and to our amazement it began to play the well-known Jewish tune, 'Hevenu Shalom Alechem'[1].

[1] *"We bring peace to you."*

Later we learned that this musical doorbell was a gift from a previous foreign visitor. Lev opened the door and laughed heartily as he saw the look of horror on our faces. Surely this tune would betray our purposes by drawing undue attention . . . "Come in" he welcomed, "Shalom alechem!"

We entered the Elberts' small two-room apartment, and were impressed at the ingenuity of Inna in utilizing every inch of space. Beds were tucked under the sofa. Curtains divided one small dining room cum study from the living room. As we sat down, Lev went to the window, opened it slightly and glanced up and down the street at the front of the apartment block. "Well done" he whispered, "you haven't picked up a tail."

Many postcards from Israel decorated the wall of the narrow hallway. Inna, Lev's wife and a cardiologist, smiled cordially. She wanted to hear all about the Third World Conference on Soviet Jewry just held in Jerusalem. We brought her hugs and kisses and very special greetings and gifts from her mother and brother in Israel. Jay and I had spent an afternoon with them just before leaving for Russia, and shared the latest family news. Inna had also prepared gifts for us to carry back to them.

Our twelve-year-old Chris was introduced to their twelve-year-old Carmi and immediately the boys disappeared into the back room to play with the new circular Rubic's cube that Chris had brought. We carried gifts of fresh coffee, chocolate, nylons and nuts.

Lev, Meridel and I began to speak, but this time with the aid of a 'magic slate'. This child's toy permitted us to speak about things we didn't want the KGB to overhear on their ubiquitous microphone system. In regular voices we would speak about the weather, the beauty of Russia and all the while we were asking questions and getting answers via the magic slate. The harsh reality of being a refusenik was everywhere.

Just two nights previously on the eve of Passover, when we were in Kiev's synagogue, the Elberts hosted a Passover seder[1] for thirty guests. Again, the second evening of Passover, they treated another thirty Jews to a typical Passover feast, complete with the reading from the Hagadah in Hebrew. The Hagadah is the order of service for the Passover meal. Also visiting Lev and Inna at this time were a doctor of physics and her teenage son from Moscow. They had travelled all night by train from Moscow so that sixteen-year-old Leonid could partake in his first Passover seder conducted with the reading of the Hagadah in Hebrew.

"Do you know a fellow named Jan Willem van der Hoeven?" Lev asked me. Laughing, I responded, "I certainly do. He is one of my best friends."

"Well, we received a Passover greeting card from him on behalf of the International Christian Embassy in Jerusalem," he grinned.

We found Lev to be a very well-informed person. He knew much of the internal and external struggles that trouble Israel. He had heard of our film "Apples of Gold" and had read about its weekly showings at the King David and LaRomme Hotels in Jerusalem. All present that afternoon were amazed and encouraged by the news of consecrated Christians who were not only standing in front of Soviet embassies around the world to cry out on their behalf, but who were

[1] 'Seder': *in this case refers to the specific order of the Passover meal which serves to remind the participants of the difficulties and the miracles associated with the Hebrew exodus from Egypt.*

fasting during Passover three days and three nights taking neither food nor water, believing as Queen Esther did for the freedom of the Jewish people. We shared that the Christian Embassy in Jerusalem held a weekly prayer meeting on Tuesday from 4 p.m. to 6 p.m. specifically for Soviet Jews, calling them out by name.

"Oh, that's when we pray here," was Lev's immediate response. There is no time change between Jerusalem and Moscow, therefore both groups were praying at the same time for many of the same things.

We also shared how our smallest son questioned why it was important for him to take a part in the demonstration for the release of Soviet Jews in front of the Knesset. He said, "Why do I have to go and cry out?" Taking him in my arms I said, "Joshua, how would you feel if you had been separated from your parents and were hated just for being who you are?" "Oh," he said hastily, "I'll go and shout." I also shared the word of the prophet Jeremiah which is found in Jeremiah 16:15-16

'The Lord liveth, that brought up the children of Israel from the land of the north, and from all the lands whither He had driven them: and I will bring them again into their land that I gave unto their father.

Behold, I will send for many fishers, saith the Lord, and they shall fish them; and after will I send many hunters, and they shall hunt them from every mountain, and from every hill, and out of the holes of the rocks.'

At the close of the conversation Lev said, "Jay, we have just received word that there is a Christian pastor in Minsk who has also been teaching this scripture verse that the Jews are going to come out of Russia in a great exodus, and he has just been admitted to a psycho-prison."

Lev gave us several good suggestions. He said that in the West we should produce and circulate a continual worldwide exhibition on Soviet Jews entitled 'The Genocide of a Culture'[1]. He made the strong request that in the future all Jews leaving Russia must go on 'aliyah' to Israel. He believes that emigration to the West actually cut off the flow of Jews leaving Russia, as unification of families in Israel was the basis on which exit visas were given. He feels that it is extremely important to teach the Jews in the USSR about their roots and therefore needs many books on the Torah and the Tenach with commentaries. He requested a commentary of Rashi on Exodus and Numbers, Hebrew prayer books. Tfillin[2] and Tallitim[2] can always be used, as well as ordinary books in Hebrew. Slides or pictures of Israel, calendars or newspapers or articles from Israel are always hungrily read here in Kiev, he said. He instructed anyone sending letters into Russia to be sure to include the post office confirmation of delivery so that they can keep track of whether the letter is delivered or not. It is of extreme importance to keep up a continual stream of letters from the free world to persecuted individuals as their existence is proof to the KGB that their plight is known abroad.

Inna's warmth and Lev's spirit challenged us to do our utmost to help them.

Again I asked, "What can we do for you?"

Lev printed his answer in capital letters on the slate, **"GIVE US A VOICE!"** These words

[1] *The film* ***"GATES OF BRASS"*** *is designed to meet this request.*
[2] *Religious objects used by Jewish men in prayer.*

immediately began to ring in my mind and from that day to this I have never forgotten the look of trust and hope in Lev and Inna's eyes.

We had no choice but to act. With this trust we continued our journey to other cities and Jewish families in Russia.

On the morning of March 31st, just hours after we had said our good-byes in Kiev, an employee of the District Military Office had delivered 'Call-up papers' to Lev which demanded that he appear at the Office for Registration. Such duty is unusual for men of Lev's age and is generally served only by high ranking officers. Years ago Lev had completed his service as a private. Such military duty would once again enable the authorities to deny his exit visa for seven additional years on the grounds of "exposure to state secrets." Nonetheless, Lev agreed to serve if he could do so in such a way that did not jeopardize his visa application, in a unit where he would not be exposed to classified information. His request was summarily denied and a summons for his military recall was issued. He asked why the summons was issued at his age. No reply was given. Refusal to comply with a summons to military duty carries a one-year prison term. Confronted with an agonizing dilemma, Lev finally decided to serve the one- year prison sentence rather than to forfeit virtually all his rights ever to emigrate to Israel.

On April 5th 1983, the day before we left the Soviet Union, we received a telephone message from Lev. He asked our new mutual friends in Leningrad, "Please ask the Rawlings to pray for us, and consider putting pressure on the Russian government concerning our case through the media."

Upon our return home to Israel we began to work for them. On May 25th there was a trial against Lev Elbert and he received a one-year prison term in a hard labour camp to begin July 3rd 1983. In June Lev made an appeal against this verdict and stated that this sentence was preventing the "re- unification of his family", a right guaranteed by the Soviet constitution.

Lev's imprisonment was actually contrary to Soviet and international law. He astutely pointed out that there was a special 'secret' order of the Ministry of Defence which limits the call-up for reserve military duty to those whose loyalty to the Soviet regime could not be questioned. Therefore, the very charges against him should have prevented his military recall. When he asked if this was correct he received the official answer that this secret order did not apply in the case of Lev Elbert. Thus, on June 16th 1983, the second trial affirmed the verdict of the first trial and on June 20th Lev started his prison term at the notorious local prison located in the outskirts of Kiev. He was in this common jail up to July 3rd when he was sent to labour camp Vinnitskaya Oblast near Kishinev in the Soviet Ukraine.

Lev arrived in this labour camp with two hundred other convicts and immediately was singled out to be searched. It must be emphasized that it was not a random selection since he was called personally by name. He was stripped and given prison garb. Later the prison officials came to his cell and informed him that there would be new and more serious charges. A package of marijuana had been found sewn into his civilian clothes. This was a frame-up! Lev had never used drugs in his life and did not even smoke. He knew KGB tactics well.

This was the way they could give him an additional sentence for three years for drug traffic. He was immediately transferred to an isolation cell reserved for 'dangerous criminals'. It was filled with homosexuals. The nightmare worsened as he was continually abused and began a hunger strike while none of his family knew what was happening to him.

Our next news of Lev was received through the following telephone call while Meridel and Joshua and I were speaking on his behalf in Toronto Canada that July. On July 18th Inna, Michael and Carmi had travelled to the labour camp and demanded to see Lev. Some of the shock and horror they experienced is evident in Inna's telephone conversation to Genya Intrator of Toronto Canada on July 31st 1983. "I have decided on a final, desperate step. Tomorrow I will start a hunger strike because I cannot stand the provocation and abuse any longer. Let everybody know about my hunger strike. Let everyone call me at my telephone number here to find out how I am. The accusation is absolutely ridiculous. Lev has never taken any drugs, not even drink or cigarettes."

"Until July 18th they refused to let us know where he was. I finally found his location through the Kiev prison and the Prosecutor's office. Lev's father, Carmi and I went to the prison camp where he told us all that had happened.

This torture and provocation is beyond human imagination. I cannot bear it any longer. To accuse my husband as a drug user is an extreme illegality. It shows that the Soviet Union has the power to do anything it wants to anyone it chooses. It can even assassinate someone in the streets if that is what it chooses to do and then make it appear perfectly legal.

They will probably disconnect my telephone but regardless of that, let the whole world know and let them call me. Let the authorities know that there are people who care. Even if my phone is disconnected, the incoming calls will be tallied by the authorities and they will know that the world knows and cares. Remind everybody that Lev's father is a very sick man. He has been through three German concentration camps so he knows what prison is like, but he completely supports me in my action.

I have never asked for anything in my whole life but I am asking you to tell the whole world to support us. Write to us, send us telegrams. Those visitors from abroad who come to Kiev, who are not afraid, let them visit me. I have reached the stage where I cannot lose anything anymore, therefore I am not afraid.

I thank you and everyone for everything you've done and are doing for us. Despite the fact that I have been absolutely sure that people will not leave me to face this most unjust fate alone, I am deeply grateful for everything. I will be very strong as you have asked me to be. I will do everything for my husband. A person must have a sense of pride, especially if he is a Jew. I wish all people would understand that what I am doing for my husband, I am not doing it only because he is my husband. He is a thoroughly honest and decent person. When they are falsely accusing him, it is just the beginning. They will be doing the same to others. They will destroy all the finest and best that we have here. They have wanted to take my husband away for many years. We don't deserve it because all we ever wanted was to go to our homeland and live with our family there, just as others have done and nothing else. That is all we ask."[1]

Inna Elbert speaks out[2]

"I am Mizrukhina, Elbert Inna Isakovna. In 1976 we applied with our entire family for an exit visa to Israel. Now my mother,my brother and about forty-two relatives are living in Israel. In 1982, after many years of being refused, we had hoped that we could leave for Israel since we received a reply from the army that no further limitations were imposed on my husband. But here our hope immediately collapsed; they began to call for additional training in the army. This placed us in the dilemma of choice: either he had to go to the army and wait for many years for a visa or he had to go to prison for a year, since a year of imprisonment is the term determined for refusal to serve. Despite our appeals to all Soviet authorities for clarification of our situation, no-one gave us an answer. He received a year's prison sentence and he was sent to a prison camp where they 'suddenly' found narcotics in his possession. Now a new case is being opened, threatening him with a term of ten years with confiscation of his entire property. And this threat, of course, stuns us. Now our entire family is subjected to this pressure. I am completely sure that there would have been neither a first nor a second trial if we had not applied for a visa to the state of Israel many years

[1] *The above telephone call from Inna Elbert in Kiev was received by Genya Intrator of Toronto, Canada, on Sunday July 31st 1983.*

[2] *Spoken by Inna Elbert in a film interview for "Gates of Brass" on November 1, 1983.*

ago to be with our relatives and close ones. No matter what happens to us, nothing can happen which would make this desire disappear. No matter how much we have to wait, all the same **WE SHALL BE IN ISRAEL.**"

Meridel and I were so moved by the experience of the Elberts that we have purposed to answer their prayer to **"GIVE US A VOICE"** by producing a film on the plight of Jewish refuseniks in the Soviet Union. Now I want to give you some factual background into the history of the plight of Jewish refuseniks before we continue with the story of the Elbert family.

2

The Hope

What is a Refusenik?

This book is not theory, rather the story of a brave group of people, the Jews, in the Soviet Union who want to go to Israel, their biblical homeland. The denial of this right by the Soviet Authorities and their refusal to grant them exit visas has birthed the term "refusenik", first coined by Michael Sherbourne in the 1970's. The thousands of Jews in Russia today who are refuseniks represent only the tip of an iceberg of traditional Russian anti-semitism. Now anti-Zionism,a subtle form of anti-semitism, has found a convenient outlet to vent Soviet hatred against the so called "hooligans, slanderers, and anti-Soviet activists". The stories in this book are true and have cost an enormous price in personal suffering and pain. Even to publish this information provides new ammunition for the KGB to harass and imprison. The reader must beware, because by fully comprehending this material you then become responsible in part for the lives of those falsely charged and innocently punished.

According to the biblical injunction in Ezekiel

33, a prophet or watchman must speak out the truth in his generation, otherwise the blood of the people is on his hands. Once he has spoken out, he is no longer held responsible. Meridel and I have felt the weight of the plight of the Soviet Jewish people. We now share that weight with you. Will you respond and fight? We believe that you will. It is of the utmost importance to see the current plight of the Soviet Jews in its historical context.

PART 1

Anti-Semitism and a brief history of Jews in Russia

A filmed interview with Professor Martin Gilbert of Oxford University, by Bruce Allen, director of ***"Gates of Brass"****. Professor Gilbert is a renowned historian, author and the official biographer of Sir Winston Churchill.*

Bruce Allen: "Tell us about the history of Russian Jewry"

Professor Gilbert: "There never really were such people as Russian Jews. There were several million Jews living in Poland and Lithuania which came under Russian rule when Russia moved westward. So Russian Jewry was a creation of Czarist expansionism under a highly extended rule over this area. The Czars then contained the Jews in what was called the "Pale of their Settlement", a large area, but one in which they were defined and confined by law.

Life in the "Pale of Settlement" was very difficult. For example, these were to a large extent poor communities, and although individuals flourished in commerce, the restrictions on them were considerable. They were refused permission to live in the capital, St. Petersburg, and in many of the other cities pogroms[1] began. And so it was that there grew up a system of enormous Jewish self-help. Finally, when the local peasants turned against them as a community of self-defence, their only way out was emigration. More than two million or one half of the Russian Jews left Czarist Russia between the first pogroms of the 1880's and the first World War. Following the mass emigration of two million or more Jews to the USA, Britain and to Palestine, as it then was, perhaps five or six million Jews came under Communist rule at the time of the Bolshevik Revolution in 1917. It was a time of great hope for them as one of the very first acts of the Bolsheviks was to abolish anti-semitism, and to abolish all of the disabilities on Jews. They were no longer confined to the "Pale of Settlement" and could speak Hebrew or Yiddish. A Jewish University was set up in 1918. The fact is that there were many Jews prominent in the Bolshevik movement and leadership, so it seemed to mean that Jewish disabilities were over. Jewish life could now flourish in the Soviet Union.

The Jew in general was never comfortable with Bolshevism, but the anti-Bolshevik forces had pursued a violent series of attacks on Jews. In 1918 and 1919 more than 100,000 Jews had been murdered in the Ukraine and Western Russia by anti-Bolshevik Russians, so Bolshevism also seemed to bring liberation and security. Of course

[1] Pogrom *is a Russian word for a violent attack against a section of the community.*

Zionism was always out in the Communist ideology. Zionist Jews were simply put on boats and deported to Palestine, which is where, after all, they wanted to be! Among those deported was Anatoly Shcharansky's uncle, Shamai Sharon, who was put on a boat in Odessa in 1920 and sent to Palestine. Quickly, however, it was clear that Communism was not an easy-going system. You followed it or you went down. Jews who had thoughts towards other systems, such as private traders, the traditional Jewish life, the small businessman or merchant, or course all fell under the Communist hand."

Question: "Describe what a 'Pogrom' is and what it might be like".

Professor Gilbert: "In the second half of the nineteenth century Jews were increasingly attacked in their homes and in their towns by mobs, often mobs of peasants roused against the Jews, sometimes roused by the Church, more often roused by the state and encouraged by the roused officials to attack Jews; to drive into the Jewish quarter of a town to smash up Jewish property; to beat Jews about the head, and in some of the pogroms ten, twenty or seventy Jews were murdered. At the time these seemed horrific figures, innocent people butchered in their beds and on the streets. In reaction to these pogroms, millions of Jews left Czarist Russia while other Jews formed self-defence organizations. Had the pogroms stopped in the 1890's perhaps Russian Jewry would have become a major factor in the later period. As it was, the pogroms continued. The notorious Kishinev Pogrom in 1903 drove hundreds of thousands more Jews out of Russia and somehow created an atmosphere in Jewish minds that Russia could never be their homeland. The few Jews who turned to Bolshevism to support Bolshevism or support the left-wing revolutionary party, although they had some support among the Jewish masses, found other Jews saying "Look this simply can't be the way out. The Russians will never accept us as Jews. We must go elsewhere, whether to America or Palestine." It was a matter of interminable debate.

Question: "1917 . . . what importance did it have to the Jews?"
Professor Gilbert: "At the beginning of 1917 the Czarist rule was in full force. Suddenly came the first "Russian Revolution" in February 1917, purporting democracy in Russia, which could have meant the end of the disabilities against the Jews and apparently there was going to be a Golden Age. This was short-lived and at the end of 1917 the second revolution, known as the "Communist Revolution" occurred. Jews were in turmoil, partly because so many Jewish individuals had played a part in this second communist revolution as its leaders. For a while it seemed even this second revolution, though it imposed communism on Russia, would maintain its refusal to persecute the Jews in any form. Of course, we now know that this was a mistake. But for two or three years the ferment of both revolutions carried on an exuberance in the Jewish world. A Jewish university was set up, all sorts of Jewish debates flourished openly and all sorts of careers, of course within the general communist ambiance, existed for Jews. Nobody pointed a finger anymore against

the Jews. The great Lenin himself condemned anti-semitism by decree, but Communism was Communism. Unfortunately the October revolution in time brought about the disabilities once again".

Question: "What is the next crucial point?"
Professor Gilbert: "There was a strange limbo period when Communism became the dominant feature of Russian life in every aspect and all citizens had to be subscribed to it, or else remain silent, whether they were Christians or Jews or held other national aspirations within the Soviet system. At the same time Yiddish, the language of most Jews, flourished, so did Yiddish publications. There was a communist encouragement of what they called the Jewish section of the Communist Party, which was intended to create a pro-communist Jewish world. But it didn't last long. Stalinism asserted itself and the purges came. Black years began for all Soviet citizens. By the time of the outbreak of the Second World War, very few Jews dared to tell their children that they were Jews, or if Jewish, what that meant".

Question: "What form did these purges take?"
Professor Gilbert: "The purges were Stalin's attempt to assert complete political power, and hundreds of thousands of Soviet citizens,some would say millions, disappeared . . . through public show trials and through executions. Nobody spoke against the regime; it was a time of silence for those who had feelings. When the war came the Jews emerged from the silence as did all Soviet citizens to defend their soil against the Nazi invader. The Jewish participation in the war was so great, not

only the Jewish suffering, not only the million and one half Jews who were murdered on Soviet soil, but Jewish participation in the war, in the fighting services, with the partisans behind the lines . . . all this Jewish participation was so remarkable that Jews felt when the war ended that the disabilities against them would also end. They would, as it were, receive, if not a reward, at least fair play in return for the part they had taken in helping to defeat Germany".

Question: "What was the anti-fascist Committee and what role did it play in the war years?"
Professor Gilbert: "Among the Jewish contribution to the Soviet war effort against the Nazis was the setting up and activity of an anti-fascist committee of Jewish writers who travelled the Western world. It came to Britain and the USA and tried to explain to Jews outside the Soviet Union that not only was the Soviet Union fighting the western battle against Hitler, and fighting it very effectively, but also that Jews, such as those on the anti-fascist committee were in the forefront of this battle. Many distinguished Jewish writers and literary figures, people like Perets Markish and Itzak Pfeffer travelled with the anti-fascist committee to the West and in a way put at ease the minds of Western and American Jews that, bad though Communism might have been in the past, now there was a common effort, Communist, Jewish and Allied against Hitler."

Question: "When the war came to an end, what happened to the idealists and their ideal?"
Professor Gilbert: "When the war came to an end,

there was a brief period when the Jewish participation was recognized. Many Jews received the highest orders for bravery. Jewish names and the Jewish story was told widely by Soviet writers including Jewish writers, but then at the very moment, ironically when the Soviet Union fought in the United Nations for the establishment of the State of Israel, which she had recognized and whose ambassador was welcomed to Moscow, at that very moment, all of the old disabilities were imposed again against the Jews. Synagogues were closed down, Jewish national aspirations were crushed and once more parents feared to say to their children, "You are a Jew", or if they knew that they were Jewish, to explain what that meant in terms of ethical code or in terms of the new State of Israel, which Russia itself had hastened to recognize".

Question: "Why the paradoxical movement of the USSR recognizing Israel and at the same time shipping Jews off to Siberia?"
Professor Gilbert: "The Soviet Union has always acted according to what it perceives its national interest to be. Clearly, national interest in 1948 was to be friendly with the new State in the Middle East. After all, the Arab states at that time were Kingdoms and Sheikdoms, and states with whom there seemed no ideological affinity at all with the Soviets. This was before the overthrow of most of their kings, whereas Israel was a new and socialist state, many of whose leaders had been born in Russia, and some of whom were left-wing Socialists. It was in the Soviet national interests to be friendly to the new State. It was equally in Soviet

national interests to suppress Jewish Zionist aspirations within the Soviet Union, because the Soviet Union internally wished to be and still wishes to be a unified state, made up of many different languages and nationalities. But if one of those nationalities wants to go elsewhere, or has thoughts outside the Soviet border, this clearly weakens the Soviet perception of themselves and must be dealt with."

Question: "After 1948 can you tell us about the time of a return to repression of Jewish Culture?"
Professor Gilbert: "The brief period after the Second World War when Jews felt their suffering and contribution in the war would bring some remuneration, passed very quickly. Within a few years all Jewish intellectuals were suppressed. The anti-fascist committee itself was destroyed and its members executed. The Soviets announced imminent arrests of Jews on account of plots alleged to be carried out by doctors and engineers against the Soviet State. Indeed, a plan was said to be afoot for the mass deportation of Jews to eastern Siberia. This never took place as the death of Stalin nipped in the bud what might have been an even more terrible period for Soviet Jews. But once more Jewishness became taboo . . . it was simply impossible to practice one's religion openly, the learning of Hebrew was out and finding out anything about Israel, except in the utmost secrecy and utmost danger, was impossible. But one thing occurred that the Soviets had not bargained for. In 1945 they had annexed the Baltic States of Lithuania, Latavia and Estonia. In Lithuania were hundred of thousands of Jews, who until the

outbreak of the Second World War had lived in democratic societies, societies in which Judiasm could be practiced openly. So, suddenly in the Soviet world, where Judiasm effectively had been banned for more than thirty years, were hundreds of thousands of Jews who could speak Yiddish and Hebrew, who knew about Zionism, who had been active in the open Zionism of the 1930's in the Baltic States, and so to the 'LOST' Jews of Soviet Russia there came the 'FOUND' Jews of the Baltic States. The mixing of the two led to a ferment and a renaissance in Jewish thought".

Question: "What was the outcome of this?"
Professor Gilbert: "This renaissance at first took a very remarkable form as there were many cities in the Soviet Union in which the Nazis had butchered hundreds of thousands of Jews: at Konar outside of Vilnius; at the Rombiuli Forest near Riga; Babi Yar in the suburbs of Kiev. To these sites hundreds and thousands of Jews came to tend the graves, to erect small monuments, to discuss among themselves not only Jewish suffering, but also Jewish aspirations; to exchange on little pieces of paper such Hebrew words as they knew, and above all to talk about Israel, the State which the Soviets said had not very long to last but which somehow seemed to be surviving. And so at these death pits and death sites active Judiasm was reborn".

Question: "Between 1950 and 1970 a new understanding came on 'who I am' to the Jewish individual".
Professor Gilbert: "The Jews were as

frightened as most Soviet citizens of the Stalinist rule of that time, but certainly the Jews also contained within their society some remnant, some inkling, of what life had been in an ethical system which was different to Communism. They had an enthusiasm for the brand new state of Israel which obviously roused Jewish aspirations in a way which had not been roused at any time since the revolution of 1917, which had seemed to throw off, momentarily, all Jewish disability. Perhaps Stalin really did fear that the establishment of the State of Israel would create within Soviet Jewry a national upsurge and ferment, which would spread to other nationalities within Russia and threaten the unified fabric, albeit the artificially unified fabric of the Soviet States".

Question: "How does shipping people off to camps differ from pogroms?"
Professor Gilbert: "Pogroms were always open; they took place in the streets; they could be seen and the key to the pogrom was to whip up the crude latent anti-semitism of simple people, to drive peasants into Jewish homes which they smashed with bricks. These were peasants who, if you left them alone, wouldn't have done it. There was something very public and artificial about a pogrom. The reactions to the pogroms by the Jews were to feel that Russia, in which they had made such contributions, in which they wished to live, against which they harboured no hostility, had turned against them.

The Stalinist policies were secretive. You disappeared; there was no publicity given to your case. Your name was erased. The great tragedy of the Stalinist era were anonymous deaths. Even now historians are researching the names of those who were picked up and disappeared.

For the majority of Jews and non-Jewish victims of the Stalinist era, one has to say his fate is unknown. He appears in a book or a document in 1936 and by 1938 he appears no more. What happened to him, we don't know. This was the era of great mystery. Nowadays it is the Western focus upon the names and faces of the people which means that we can monitor their fate from hour to hour. This is in the view of many Soviet Jews trapped in Russia today their great defence. The Stalinist period was a time of anonymity but today their names and faces are know and this protects them".

PART 2

Anti-Zionism – Soviet-Style Propaganda

Zionism, in simple terms, is a movement to reunite the Jewish people with the land of Israel. This is not a popular concept. From time immemorial, forces of anti-semitism have used various ways and means to attack the Jews and their biblical homeland, Israel. The latest has combined the Soviets and the United Nations in an alliance of lies. The objectives of this anti-Zionist hate campaign are four-fold:

(i) To delegitimize the ideal of Zionism as racist and fascist.

(ii) To slander Jews world-wide.

(iii) To defame the nation of Israel.

(iv) To discredit Jews in the Soviet Union and thereby sanction the continual attack on Russian Jews wanting to go to Israel.[1]

On November 10th 1975 a resolution was passed in the UN General Assembly by one hundred and thirteen votes to seventeen with fifteen abstensions, determining that "Zionism is a form of racism". Since that date there has been an annual UN ritual of condemnation of Israel and Jews world-wide as "Zionists", the harbingers of world instability. According to the 1978 UN Commission for the Rights of Man in general, Zionism has been condemned as "an affront to humanity". This theme was picked up by the Conference of Non-Aligned Countries in Cuba in 1979 which called Zionism "a crime against humanity"[1]. The Soviet propaganda machine has conveniently linked ancient anti-semites and modern anti-Zionism to serve their global purposes. Now these concepts are used virtually interchangeably. Once Zionism was reduced to racism it gave license to anti-semitism on a much wider scale. Now Zionism, Judiasm and Jews could be linked with the inhumane and internationally unacceptable concept of racism. The voting record in the UN of Third World nations against Israel, 95% of the time, proves the success of the Russian propaganda tool in the international arena.

Zionists, the Holocaust and Nazism

During the years following World War Two people were in a state of shock due to the horrific reports of the Holocaust. The Nazi excesses were perhaps worst of all in the Soviet Union where

[1] *Amipaz, Gitta: "Jews in the Soviet Union" Information Briefing. Israel Information Center, Jerusalem, pages 8, 9.*

millions of Jews and Russians died at their hands. This caused the Russian propaganda to gear up in a strange way. The Russians pointed out that in the '50's and '60's all problems in the USSR were linked to the effects of fascist Nazis and "western cosmopolitans". At the time it was not as popular to denounce the Jews. However, by the '70's and '80's it was convenient to link the "Zionist fascists" with the "U.S. imperialists" in their aspirations to rape the free world of goods and territory. The war in Lebanon became an ideal place in which to "nazify" Israeli Zionists. Cartoons in the Russian newspaper Pravda showed Israeli soldiers blocking off Lebanon with barbed wire and calling it "Auschwitz". To the Soviets Zionism has become modern fascism. This paranoia is clearly evident and growing in Russian publications in the cold war period of the '80's.

In 1982 L. Korneev published a book in the U.S.S.R. entitled, "The Class Nature of Zionism". According to this "expert" Zionism is the accursed enemy of progress. He states that it co-operated with the Nazis annihilating European Jewry and in one area of the Ukraine the Zionists were in co-operation with the Hitlerites and destroyed half a million Jews. He said that in fact European Jewry was wiped out by the Nazis in co- operation with the Zionists! Korneev is also the editor of the paper for students produced by Pravda Newspaper in Moscow entitled "The Pioneer", specially for children aged ten to fourteen years old. In this new book Korneev states that anti-semitism is not a result of Russian or religious problems but only Jewish greed. He very carefully re-writes the history of World War Two and states that Hitler paid Jews to leave Nazi Germany. He also states that it was the Zionists who initiated the massacres of hundreds of thousands of Jews in World War Two because they were not needed for the new state.

This circle of lies and deception has now evolved to the point where even the Holocaust is considered a lie, a fabrication, a Jewish invention. This false concept was published in a book by Korneev's colleague, Professor A.Katz, entitled "The Lie of the 20th Century". It is hard to believe the extent to which Russian propagandists will go to dupe their public. It is important for people in the free world to be aware of the techniques used by Communist propaganda. To the Soviet Communist party, the end justifies the means. Closely allied with the KGB, the Soviet Department of Propaganda, is the official organ through which the Communist party guides it's world-wide propaganda program. It utilizes four main techniques:

(i) Deception by distorting and misrepresenting facts.
(ii) Implying guilt by association instead of direct accusation.
(iii) Repetition of certain key words and claims.
(iv) Redirecting popular sentiment away from what the government regards as undesirable towards something acceptable.

These techniques are used in the written word, lectures, films and on television.[1]

World-wide slander of Zionists

The Soviet writer previously mentioned

[1] *Leon, Dan: "Battling anti-Zionism" article published in the Jerusalem Post, January 13th, 1985, page 8.*

L.Korneev asks in the December 10th 1980 issue of Komosomalskaya Pravda, a newspaper for teenagers, "What is Zionism?" To answer he writes, "One of its main ideas is formulated in the slogan, 'Jew, your country stretches from the Nile to the Euphrates.' Who put forth this mad idea? It was the Great Jewish bourgeousie . . . to become even richer and more influential. This is why Zionism has extended its power over all citizens of Jewish origin, whether they be in the U.S. Italy, France, West Germany or any other country. Even the trademark of blue jeans, "Levi", participates in their operation; the profits from the sale of these trousers are used to help Zionists. Most monopolies of arms manufacturers are controlled by Jewish bankers . . . the bombs which kill in Lebanon enrich the bankers Hazard and Hold. Bandits choke the life out of schoolboys in Afghanistan and the coffers of Lehman and Guggenheim fill up. Zionism is the fascism of our time".[1]

The lashing out of Soviet authorities against the Jews moves in cycles. Chameleon-like, Russian policy is always manipulated to serve its own purposes and create the desired effect at any given moment. A good illustration of this occurred in 1948. The Soviet Government supported the UN Partition resolution that gave rise to the creation of the State of Israel. This policy was established in an effort to undermine the British presence in the Middle East. The Soviets were delighted when the British pulled out of Palestine, and even for a short while supported Israel's successful military efforts against its Arab neighbours. It meant the

[1] *Leon, Dan; "Battling anti-Zionism" article published in the Jerusalem Post, January 13th 1985, page 8.*

establishment of a "socialist", albeit weak, government in the midst of militant, dictatorial kingdoms and sheikdoms of the Arab Middle East. Andrei Gromyko, as Soviet representative at the UN of May 13th 1948, the day before the establishment of the State of Israel, said, "as to the aspirations of the Jews to establish their own state, it would be unjust not to take this, the Holocaust, into consideration and to decry the right of the Jewish people to realize this aspiration".[1] Unfortunately this policy did not last for long.

Since 1967 Soviet anti-semitism, now termed anti-Zionism, became progressively more hateful. The one scapegoat term of Communist propaganda "cosmopolitans or Western capitalists" had been overworked in the media and a new target was needed. This transition became more and more necessary since the ubiquitous "black market" or underground capitalist system that operates clandestinely throughout the Soviet Union needed to be down-played. The obvious group to attack were the Jews; that is the world-wide network of rich U.S.-backed Jewish imperialists. It was published that Zionists had collaborated with the Nazis in the Holocaust and, in fact, were "fascists" in disguise. They were accused of being successors to the Nazis by committing genocide of the Arabs in Palestine and Lebanon. The ancient libel of the "Protocols of the Elders of Zion", a proven fake publication, indicated that the Jewish religion inspires its adherents to seize control of the world and destroy other people. Through calculated propaganda the Soviets have made Zionism, Racism, Judaism and Israel interchangeable,

[1] *Leon, Dan: "Battling anti-Zionism" article published in the Jerusalem Post, January 13th 1985, page 8.*

thereby resurrecting anti-semitism on a global scale.[1]

Attempts to discredit Soviet Jews and their aspirations to emigrate to Israel

Russian socialism and Israeli socialism proved to be poles apart. In 1948 Golda Meir arrived in Moscow as the first Israeli ambassador to the U.S.S.R. The enthusiastic welcome of the Soviet Jews hardly knew any bounds. On her attendance at the synagogue in Moscow on the High Holy Days she experienced the joy, pride and love of the Jewish masses by kisses and hugs as she represented Israel, her own people. Finally, after all the years of terror and persecution, Russian Jewry could identify with a free nation that gave them hope for the future. Golda exclaimed, "Praise God, that we could live so long to see such a glorious day". The euphoria was short-lived. Stalin, in his aging paranoia, viewed the Jewish nationalist aspirations as a threat to "Mother Russia" and set about to destroy the disloyalty of the Jews lest it spread to other national minorities. Stalin embarked on those barbaric acts that caused his last half decade of power to be called "The Black Years". Once again the Russian Jewish Community was caught in a death struggle.

On the one hand in 1948 Soviet policy towards Israel was positive, since it helped the overall global strategy of the Communists. This gave the local Jewish population hope, especially in light of the courage and valour of the Jews in helping to defeat the military forces of Hitler. However, their hopes were soon dashed and new anti-semitic

[1] *Amipaz, Gitta: "Jews In The Soviet Union" Information Briefing. Israel Information Center, Jerusalem, pages 8, 9.*

attacks made the sting even greater, in spite of the fact that the Soviet regime needed the Jewish intelligensia in the sciences, arts and economics to help rebuild Russia in the post Stalin years. On the one hand Jews and Israel were needed, but deep rooted anti-semitism could not be eradicated from the very fabric of Russian society.

Defamation of the State of Israel

The Soviets go to great lengths to defame Israel and Zion. In fact they are fighting the Scriptures. Zion, according to the Bible has a fourfold meaning.

(1) Zion is the Land of Israel.

Psalm 69:35	Isaiah 35:10
Psalm 102:13,16	Isaiah 51:3,11
Psalm 132:13	Isaiah 64:10
Psalm 133:3	Jeremiah 30:17
Psalm 128:5	Jeremiah 50:5
Psalm 134:3	Jeremiah 3:14
Psalm 137:1,3	Jeremiah 31:6,12
Isaiah 34:8	Amos 1:2
Isaiah 40:8,9	Micah 4:2
Isaiah 52:7,8	Zechariah 8:2,3
Isaiah 66:8	Zechariah 1:14,17
Isaiah 14:32	

(2) Zion is a hillock in the city of Jerusalem.

II Samuel 5:7	Isaiah 10:12
I Kings 8:1	Isaiah 24:23
I Chronicles 11:15	Isaiah 29:8
II Chronicles 5:2	Isaiah 31:4
Psalm 2:6	Isaiah 33:20
Psalm 20:2	Isaiah 41:27
Psalm 48:2,11,12	Isaiah 52:1

Psalm 51:18
Psalm 74:2
Psalm 78:68
Psalm 110:2
Psalm 125:1
Psalm 135:21
Psalm 149:2
Isaiah 2:3
Isaiah 4:5
Isaiah 8:18
Isaiah 18:7
Isaiah 60:14
Isaiah 62:1
Lamentations 5:18
Joel 2:32
Obadiah 17,21
Micah 4:2,7
Zechariah 1:14,17
Isaiah 37:32
Revelation 14:1

(3) Zion is the Jewish People.

Psalm 14:7
Psalm 53:6
Psalm 97:8
Psalm 126:1
Psalm 129:5
Psalm 146:10
Isaiah 1:27
Isaiah 12:6
Isaiah 33:5
Isaiah 40:8,9
Isaiah 49:14
Isaiah 51:16
Isaiah 52:7,8
Isaiah 59:20
Jeremiah 9:19
Joel 2:23
Joel 3:16
Zechariah 9:13
Romans 9:33
Romans 11:26

(4) Zion is also a reference to heaven.

Hebrews 11:22

Soviet and Arab propagandists have singled out Israel in cold harsh terms as "the Zionist entity". Israeli foreign policy makers and Israeli Defence Forces are routinely described as "Zionist aggressors" and "criminal expansionists" in the Soviet press. On the very day after the Israeli Defence Forces began to liberate Beirut from the total destruction and desecration of the PLO terrorists and Syrian occupation forces, the official Soviet news agency announced on June 15th 1982 that "Tel Aviv has embarked on a criminal path of genocide in an attempt to put a bloody end to the struggle of the Palestine people . . . " The report went on to point out "Washington's complicity in the Israeli aggression" and stressed that Israel's attack on a sovereign Arab nation was the product of stategic co-operation between the U.S. and Israel . . . it went on that "the Israeli military, with Washington's blessing, went on to capture West Beirut after the Palestine terrorists had left the city and engineered a bloodbath". All the above is completely erroneous as Israeli Defence Forces only went into Lebanon after twelve years of restraint. They watched Lebanon being systematically destroyed by PLO terrorists, Muslim extremist factions, and subsequently by Syrian so called 'peace-keeping troops'. In addition the northern border of Israel in the Galilee region was continually subjected to terrorist artillery shellings and rocket attacks. Conditions became unbearable as large portions of the society were forced to spend countless night in bomb shelters. The nearly continuous disruption of civil and economic life became unbearable. Israel had to act and clear a "cordon sanitare" in South Lebanon free of PLO terrorists. When the Israeli troops entered Lebanon at first they were received as liberators, and only because they found such great quantities of Russian-supplied arms did they realize that they had to eliminate the PLO terrorists from all of Lebanon, including Beirut, in order to ensure safety for its northern citizens on the borders of Lebanon.

The actual facts of the horrific civil war that

decimated the county of Lebanon were never completely told in the world press. The real story is included in our book "Fishers and Hunters". We also have the filmed Lebanese response to the Israeli responses to the Israeli Defence Forces in our half-inch video production entitled, "Lebanon and the Middle East, The Untold Story". Both this book and the video are available by using the order form on the last page.

Our response to Soviet lies

Meridel and I were shocked at the extent of anti-Israel propaganda in the Soviet press and radio. While we were in Moscow in March and April 1983, we were amazed at the blatant lies we heard and read. It was reported on Moscow radio on April 3rd 1983 that the Israeli Zionists had used chemical warfare against the "innocent Palestinians by pouring poison into their wells on the West Bank". We spoke back into the speaker of the radio in the hotel room hoping that it also held hidden microphones, which is the usual practise, and said loudly, "You are liars! This is not the truth!"

Another interesting event took place during the "Esther Fast". It was a "first-of-its-kind" Russian television program. A communist Jewish General named Dragunsky, a man influential in military circles, appeared on television after the 7:00 p.m. national news broadcast. He painstakingly explained why Zionism is a force that must be severely dealt with. He instructed his prime-time viewers that they needed to be on the alert for any Zionist activities in their neighbourhoods, and instructed that offending Jews should be reported to the authorities at once. Dragunsky was one of many puppets who signed an article entitled "The Appeal" which denounced their own people as Zionist and traitors.

Dr. Alexander Luntz, a former refusenik and mathematician now living in Israel said, "An honest man would not have signed this article. The Soviets use those who are on the hook and are afraid not to sign".

From the above it is obvious that the Russians will go to any length to strike down the Jews. A television program, entitled "Traders of Souls" also verified the 'Zionists' and refuseniks as traitors and criminals. Can we continue to allow these untruths to go unchallenged? Definitely not. When we visited the refuseniks in Moscow and Leningrad we were challenged to give them a chance to speak for themselves and began to work immediately for a practical way to accomplish this. Out of this the concept of a film production was conceived.

Concept of a film is born

I have never forgotten their sincere faces and parting words, "Please give us a voice. If you don't speak up now, it will be too late". With these words ringing in my soul I knew I had to help. In response we have made a one-hour film and documentary entitled, "Gates of Brass" to express internationally the plight of these modern-day heroes. Thanks to people just like you, funds have come in from all over the world to pay for this non-profit production. We believe it is our responsibility at home and abroad to stand up and be counted for the cause of truth and righteousness on the earth. We who have an opportunity to speak must not be guilty of silence. Proverb 31:8,9 says:

'Speak up for those who cannot speak for themselves, for the rights of all who are destitute.

Speak up and judge fairly, defend the rights of the poor and needy'.

Here are some of the quotes from these very courageous Jewish men and women who willingly spoke out against the injustices of the Soviet system. Will you too speak out?

"Give us a voice"

"The frightening ghosts of Nazi Germany have risen from their graves".

"If you don't speak up now, it will be too late".

"Authorities will tolerate no Jewish cultural activity".

"Tiredness is accumulating, the tiredness of hopelessness".

"Anti-semitism is the eleventh plague".

"When they begin to centralize us, you will know the end is near".

"We are facing a spiritual break-down; our faces are crushed to the wall until blood flows".

"Police agents who were photographing our children spoke some Hebrew".

"My life as a refusenik has been my most

important and creative period".

"We are overcoming our enemies".

"History is being made today but it doesn't just depend on us. Our common history is made by joined hands".

"Please read the Psalms for us".

"God is building the life of a man beautifully, if that man tries to serve him, even if a man does not realize it. Man must see this beauty with God's help".

"Sometimes, I have a sad feeling, which can be expressed through the words found in Rahshi's commentary on Genesis 17:8 which says, 'A Jew outside of Israel is as if he has no God at all' ".

In hearing them make these statements, we declared to them that the days of un-involvement and silence are over. Please back up our words with your actions. You can help give them a voice. Together we can proclaim:

"Freedom for the captives, and release for the prisoners"
Isaiah 61:1

PART 3

Our Observations

The following information was recorded by Meridel in her personal diary as we travelled through the Soviet Union in March and April 1983.

Moscow

"Eight million Russian people live within the confines of Moscow. We are told she hosts three million visitors annually. During our stay we met Ethiopians studying medicine and Palestinians from the old city of Jerusalem training to be fighter pilots. We saw visitors from India, Pakistan, Japan, Albania, Hungry, Czechoslovakia, Poland, Germany, Armenia, Europe, and many parts of the Soviet Union itself as well as North America. We heard Arabic spoken frequently. Many of the visitors from Third World nations were left wide-eyed by the glories displayed to them in this, the capital of the 'greatest power'. We could not help but wonder if somehow we in the 'Christian West' have not failed our brothers in the Third World nations by not extending ourselves to aid in their individual education and national development to the same degree as the Soviet Union has. Obviously, through her propaganda and assistance programs "Mother Russia" has birthed untold numbers of dedicated children in countries around thc world.

We remained in Moscow throughout the three days of the world-wide Esther fast, April 1, 2 and 3, learning many things. Seventy American cents equalled one Russian rouble according to the official bank rate. But we were told that one could buy five roubles for one American dollar on the Russian black market. Average people on the streets or in the restaurants approached us, asking to buy our watches, jeans, coats, t-shirts, cameras – anything. One pound of coffee sells for U.S.$60.00 on the black market. We did not fail to notice that the large store windows in downtown Moscow were virtually empty except for a piece of Indian fabric hung in an artistic way and perhaps fifty cans of sardines piled high. Most of the buildings had not seen any fresh paint for decades and outside of the city the majority of highways in the U.S.S.R. are unpaved and are lined with houses built in the pre-revolutionary days.

Generally the people appeared to be depressed and would avoid direct eye contact. Rarely were we offered a friendly smile or hello other than in homes of refuseniks. Fear, intimidation and suspicion seemed to rule every individual. One never hears a person singing or whistling in the street. Grocery and shoe stores evoked the longest queues. At times there was no milk for sale.

Our contact for Moscow had been arranged in the home of Lev Elbert by friends visiting him from Moscow. They were Inna and her teenage son, Leonid. We agreed to meet at the Bolshoi Ballet Theatre on the day of our arrival in Moscow. They took us to their apartment entrance and as we entered I silently offered up the following prayer. 'Oh, Lord, these people who are so noble and highly educated have to live in such filthy and dreary surroundings. Would you kindly control the expression on my face that I in no way respond to the ghastly smell that I am now smelling. Amen'. There was a rubbish shoot in their building that smelled like a chicken house so that when one entered the building you were almost suffocated by this horrific sense of filth. However, when we arrived inside their apartment and closed the door we were in a little sanctuary. Inna's husband is a doctor of mathematics now working only as a special tutor. Inna is a PhD physicist, also jobless.

They have been refused a visa for several years as their oldest son applied first for an exit visa and this produced the loss of his father's job in the Moscow University and later his mother's research position.

Inna's husband said that as a private tutor they make enough money to live and they do not need to worry about the rent as they own their apartment. He said, smiling, 'We live like the birds, by faith, in the midst of this Communist 'Utopia'. 'Everyone here suffers', the doctor continued, 'the Soviets are terrible to their own Russian people'. Facing Jay he added, 'How do you live'?

'Well', said Jay, 'I guess we're not the typical product of a capitalist society as we have willingly given up our means of livelihood to serve the Lord for fifteen years now. We have lived by faith just like you, Doctor'. We all chuckled at the irony of the situation. Then, looking at us seriously and folding his hands, the doctor leaned on the table and whispered 'Things are getting worse. When they begin to centralize us, you'll know the end is near'. His eyes were intelligent, grave and sad.

Chris, our son, turned out to be a very unique blessing for this family because he was a good example of a child brought up in Israel, having lived there for half of his twelve years. He and Leonid disappeared and Inna explained that they had gone shopping. The boys' conversation was carried out in English interspersed with a few Hebrew words. They both seemed to enjoy each other's company and had a very relaxed and happy time, for when they returned home that were as casual and carefree as any two boys anywhere in the world. Leonid had taken Chris into a large department store and purchased for him a hockey game as he has discovered that this was one of Chris's favourite sports. It was so difficult to receive this expensive gift from these dear friends who have many needs themselves.

In response, Chris quickly shed his new 'Alligator trademark' shirt and gave it to Leonid. We then took a photo of the two grinning boys, one holding a hockey game and the other displaying his new shirt.

Over endless cups of tea we shared the news of what was happening in Jerusalem and Israel. There were individual messages from family members in Israel and gifts to be delivered. Our biggest job was to continually re-assure these 'refuseniks' that they were not a forgotten people, that the world knew of their plight. Most were surprised to learn of a biblical basis for their future exodus promised by their Jewish prophets. We did our best to encourage them. They were amazed. By this time a lady named Natasha dropped in for tea with her two younger daughters. We brought her hugs and very special greetings from Dina, her very close friend of many years, now working as an aeronautical engineer in Israel. Dina had sent a large bottle of 'Johnny Walker' whisky with us for Natasha. When we set it on the table in front of her she laughed and said, 'I had some reservations about you Christians, but now I know that you are really real!' She had a very special need for the whisky.

Natasha is a 'mother in Israel' in the USSR, so to speak. She has a very special task that keeps her in close touch with Jewish prisoners and uses the whisky to bribe the prison guards to allow her people to receive letters, special medicines, even gifts. She sends food parcels twice a year, as permitted by Soviet law and packs them carefully and creatively. She was delighted with the quantity and variety of health foods we brought from friends in Europe. Natasha is a woman known for her courage and selflessness.

Just recently news had reached Dina in Jerusalem that Natasha had been registered as an eternal refusenik and must not apply again for her visa to Israel. Jay carefully asked her how she felt about it and she simply threw back her head and laughed saying 'Ha, what does this country know about eternity'?

Natasha's husband, an observant Jew, is also a refusenik and just recently received word that his mother had died in Israel. His request to fly to her funeral was flatly refused.

We all went by subway to the apartment of another family of refuseniks. This contact had been arranged for us by Genya Intrator, former head of the Canadian Committee for Soviet Jewry. We had a very warm time of sharing and they were not afraid of speaking frankly in their home with some careful reservations. So we arranged by 'magic slate' where to have our next meeting in the open air.

Our many days in Moscow quickly filled with visits morning, noon and night in the homes of refuseniks. We met a courageous and humourous people who treated us as their very own. They insisted that we eat their food and meet their friends. Their hospitality was the warmest of any nation we have visited. After listening to their heartaches such as young people who at the age of fourteen must make the very difficult decision of whether or not to join the 'Young Pioneer' youth movement in Russia which embodies the Communist doctrine, in refusing to join they automatically seal their fate. They will never have the privilege of higher education and will always be limited to menial labour tasks upon completion of high school. We met a people of faith, a people who are still being sorely tried and tested. Perhaps we were most amazed by their sense of personal freedom. They had chosen to be Jews. They were not just biological Jews. They were Jews who were real and committed to the survival of their people. They were aware of the world in which they were living and have few illusions about the terrible possibilities of their future. But in spite of their daily suffering we found them experiencing the joy of the Lord with a good sense of humour. The stories they wanted to hear from us most were 'faith stories'. They were intrigued to hear of our travels from nation to nation with three little boys and to hear how the Lord healed our sicknesses and met our every need along the way. They wanted to know in fine detail what life is really like in Israel. Most were quite amazed that the word of God says that He is going to make a provision for their release. We did our best to instill an inspiration and faith in the Almighty that no system will ever deny them of, a faith that will help them hold on while all the odds are against them. Many said to us, 'Friends bring us many gifts but you have brought us hope'.

It was very late one night in the home of another family. The room was filled with Jews listening to the stories Jay was telling about the world wide actions on their behalf, actions that not only involved governments and media but actions that involved many individuals through their own fastings and prayers. One lady leaned over to me and said, 'What is it that we feel when your husband is speaking? What is it? He is obviously telling us the truth, it gives me chills.'

At the end of the 'Esther Fast' on April 3rd Jay asked a group of mathmeticians, economists, engineers and doctors, 'Has anyone seen any changes during the last few days'? We were interested in their answer. An engineer confirmed that for the first time he was able to receive 'The Voice of America' and the B.B.C. on short wave without KGB electronic jamming. This was very significant for thousands were fasting and praying all over the world exactly at that time sending prayers out over Russia. All agreed that

'We wrestle not against flesh and blood, but against principalities, against powers, against the rulers of the darkness of this world, against spiritual wickedness in high places'.

Ephesians 6:12

Our last day in Moscow was spent with a young married couple, Sergei and Ella, who have been refuseniks for nine years. They were delivered exit visas and then stopped at the airport as they were leaving the country for Israel. Soviet government officials said, 'Your visas have been revoked'. Since then they have never been given an explanation why they were refused. The stock answer has been 'because you were refused last time'.

We were very, very touched by their simplicity and sincerity. Sergei greeted the three of us warmly and ushered us into his one-room apartment. We did not fail to notice the wallpaper peeling from the walls nor the broken rocking chair in the corner nor the frayed Israeli sandals on his feet. No sooner were we seated than he served us each a cup of coffee. We noticed that it had been sent to him from Israel. 'I am so glad that you have come. Last night my wife and I were almost ready to give up, we were so discouraged. But you have come today and we see it as a good sign. Ella is just out shopping,' her husband explained. 'When she returns we will eat lunch'.

Jay protested immediately, 'Oh, Sergei, we have not come to eat. Please, we've just come to see you both'.

At that moment Ella returned, bearing two precious oranges in her hand. In spite of the lack of food, we sat down to a lovely meal. First we were served boiled potatoes and then a sardine. This was served with more Israeli coffee and matzah. The two oranges were cut five ways and served for dessert. This Scripture from Psalm 23 kept running through my head in relation to my friend's seemingly fragile existence amongst such hatred.

'Thou preparest a table before me in the presence of mine enemies'.

I must say that Chris and Jay and I were close to tears.

In our conversation we found out that Ella is a linguist and speaks many languages perfectly. Sergei is an historian on the 17th and 18th century Russian history and has been working as a tour guide to make ends meet. He is also a teacher of Hebrew and holds Hebrew classes in his home once a week. He begged us to stay that we might address his students. He also suggested that we meet Anatoly Shcharansky's brother and mother. Time was against us. Sergei was the second person who shared with us the good news that he had been able to hear the BBC and the 'Voice of America' on short wave radio late at night. Again, he said it was a first. We shared with him the good news of Christian action world-wide on their behalf as we had to many of our other refusenik friends. Sadly, Sergei and Ella felt that they had been forgotten by their own. Sergei spoke very carefully about recognizing the tricks of the KGB and warned that they have people who are false refuseniks who continually give the party line in public statements.

Ella blessed us all before leaving to go back to our hotel when she presented us with a brand new candle and said, 'Please take this back to Israel and tell our friends there and in the West that the light has not gone out in Russia'.

That night as the sun was setting over the Kremlin we stood on one side of Red Square and walked to the other,praying as we went, agreeing with God's people around the world that He would release His ancient Jewish people out of the grips of the Russian 'Bear'.

Leningrad

The Lord has a good sense of humour. No sooner had our plane taxied onto the runway in Leningrad and cut off its engines, including air conditioning, when the following song began to play over the P.A. system: 'By the rivers of Babylon we sat down and wept when we remembered Zion'. The many Russian passengers abroad this 'Aeroflot' plane sat contentedly tapping their feet to the upbeat music.

We were excited, listening to the words 'May the words of my mouth and the meditations of my heart be acceptable in Your sight, O Lord'. Jay whispered in my ear, 'that one certainly slipped past the censors!.

We visited in the home of refuseniks Pinchas and Sonya, who were also discouraged. As a young married couple they were experiencing much opposition and tension in their relationships with their parents because they had chosen to become observant Jews. Sonya, who was expecting her first child, was on pregnancy leave and Pinchas, a former engineer, is now bagging groceries in a local store. We sang them some of the songs of Zion and read a poem that had been especially written for the refuseniks from Jerusalem by Yoma Munting.

Remember Naphtali

We touch you tenderly
with our thoughts and prayers
within the prisons of despair and gloom
and though you feel deserted, alone,
your sighs, your groans
are heard
by him who cares
infinitely.

Remember Naphtali –
a hind let loose,
Father, may it be – speedily.

Be sure
that within the confines of your pain,
your soul has been sculptured
sacredly,

your heart enlarged.
For, as we stroke your cheek again,
sensitively,
we are melted, scalded.
Father . . . speedily!
Father . . . Naphtali!

Your reality, so stark and bleak,
your sighs, like wind through soaking rain
compel us seek
your release –
as a hind
bounding over hills and plains
towards
a peaceful lake.

They were visibly moved and shared with us the problem, the very real problem of assimilation of Jews in the USSR They requested that we send them books such as 'The Art Scroll' series on the Bible and Jewish history as well as the Menorah series of instructional books on Judaism. They also requested Hebrew newspapers.

Our final contact was not made until 10:00pm the last night were were in Leningrad. From our hotel we walked to Ya'acov's apartment block. It had been an exhausting trip and we were bone weary. Upon entering his very neat apartment, Chris stretched out on the sofa and fell soundly asleep. We were impressed by the large flannelgraph hanging in Ya'acov's living room portraying the story of Queen Esther with large Hebrew writing. He explained that several families in Leningrad had planned to hold a Purim party for their children in

March at Ya'acov's home. However, the KGB got wind of it and planted themselves outside of his apartment door, allowing no one to enter. Ya'acov shrugged his shoulders and said, 'We still haven't had the party, but we will have, one day'.

I noticed that Ya'acov kept glancing towards Chris with such a longing as if he wanted to go over and tenderly hold him and hug him. I did not understand what I was seeing. It was later, over hot mugs of sweet Russian tea, served with homemade cranberry jam on top of matzah that Jay spied a map of New York spread out on the living room floor. Ya'acov shared his story with us.

Several years ago, Ya'acov and his family had applied for exit visas to Israel. Because of his profession as a nautical engineer he had supposedly gained access to state secrets and could not be allowed out of the country. However his family, including his wife and two dear teenage children were given a choice: to leave without Ya'acov or stay forever. This meant that his wife would have to divorce him or to stay in Russia with him where his children had no future. It was a heart-wrenching decision because of their love for each other. Finally, however he decided to divorce his wife and thereby permit them to go to freedom. Presently the children, now nineteen and twenty years old, are studying in college in New York and upon graduation plan to go to Israel. All of a sudden I realised the longing that I had seen in Ya'acov's face as he looked toward our sleeping son.

We were especially touched by his life of dedication to the cause of his people. Ya'acov holds special lectures on traditional Jewish subjects and was very eager for any information that we could leave with him. He specifically requested a Bible, preferably in Russian or English, and he needs materials to make up gift packages for refuseniks in prison. It was after midnight and we wept as we left Ya'acov and went on our way to freedom. If you would like to write to Ya'acov, please contact us.

Tension!!!

The entire Soviet system is designed to produce intimidation and fear. It is hard to surmount when one is innocent but it is much more difficult when one has some degree of involvement. Upon our arrival at the Leningrad airport for our flight to Helsinki, we found the security and customs officials very busy indeed. The American Jewish friends that we had met on the tour bus the previous day were being harassed to put it mildly. All of their luggage was searched, pulled apart and examined very closely while they were continually questioned. Before they could go to freedom they were relieved of their address book with seventy names and addresses of refuseniks, plus all of their film and photographs including those of their grandchildren. In contrast our bags simply passed through the x-ray machines unopened.

As I stood at the passport office waiting for Jay to be cleared from the money changer, the panic that filled the room also affected me. Two businesslike men came running through the customs waving their passports. One shouted, 'Which way to passport control?' I waved my hand giving direction and out of my mouth slipped the word, 'Bavakasha' which is Hebrew for 'if you please'. I threw my hand over my mouth in disbelief and prayed, 'Oh, Lord, my mind has snapped under the pressure'.

As the young businessman passed me, I was further amazed by his incredible response, 'Todah rabah!' which is Hebrew for 'thank you'.

Only later during our flight into freedom did these two gentlemen make themselves known to us as young rabbis from America who had also been visiting 'the family'. Upon hearing this I said, 'see, I knew you in the Spirit!'. 'Yes', he replied, 'we met at Mount Sinai'.

3

The Cry

Gifts to Russia

'Withhold not good from them to whom it is due, when it is in the power of thine hand to do it.'
Proverbs 3:27

I now want to give you some background as to how our interests grew in Soviet Jewry. In July, 1972, we were thrilled when the Lord began to speak to a group of us to make a trip to the USSR to help the Jews who were hopeful of going to Israel. Plans were made and a tour group arranged.

Fifty-two people set out on a most unusual tour. As we prepared to embark on this journey, we knew the most important thing was to hear from the Lord as to His plans for us, not our own. In prayer the Lord showed several of us that we were to do four things. First, to take our Jewish friends in Russia Hebrew language teaching materials, and secondly, the words of the biblical prophets so that they could understand that the final authority over their fate is the not the Communist Party but God Almighty. Thirdly, we were to take a letter and petition to Premier Brezhnev who was in power at the time, in which we clearly pointed out the dismay of people in the West in response to the Soviet treatment of their citizens, especially the Jews. Also outlined in the letter were the scriptures from Jeremiah, Isaiah and the Psalms showing that the Jews would one day be released. Fourth, we were to visit Red Square and stand before Lenin's Tomb and the Kremlin, the seat of Communist power, to pray and speak a prophetic word of release **"North give up. Let my People go".** As we made plans for this trip to Russia we also included a week-long visit to Israel.

Our journey from North America took us through Denmark and Finland. While in Helsinki we were able to locate several hundred Bibles in Russian. We had the Hebrew teaching materials with us. Our group was made up of an assortment of teenagers, middle-aged and older people. One lady was in a wheelchair. We entered Russia through Leningrad. Each person had his share of small Bibles hidden on his person. The teenagers thought it was a great adventure as they tucked Bibles into their togs and nonchalantly walked through Soviet customs. I remember a heart-stopping experience as I had much of the Hebrew language materials, all forbidden by the Soviets, in one of two identical suitcases. The customs officer pointed directly at the suitcase in which the Hebrew materials were packed. I gulped and under my breath said a quick prayer for help. Just then the customs officer was distracted by a commotion in another part of the hall and I quickly substituted the "clean" suitcase. He opened it and told us to go on.

We rode the bus from the airport to the hotel and word was spread from one to another to rendezvous one by one in our room. We would collect all the Bibles into one place. It was dangerous to leave them lying around in suitcases as the KGB would search our bags when we went out to tour. Finally we got all the Bibles together and loaded them into a suitcase. The suitcase then went with us everywhere. Never was it let out of our sight. When asked what it was we simply smiled and said "important documents". The KGB knew that we carried all our airplane tickets in one case, so they weren't too suspicious.

Upon our arrival in Leningrad we were tired and nearly everyone went to bed early; all except one very zealous young man from Boston. He had cleverly photocopied a portion of scripture, John 3:16 out of one of the Russian Bibles before we left Helsinki. He went out on the street and foolishly began to give out his "little gifts". At once the police arrested him and took him to KGB headquarters. There he was interrogated and our group leader was called in to explain this "unacceptable activity" . We were forced to promise that no more "gifts" would be given out in Russia, on the threat that if this type of activity occured again, we would all be sent out on the next available plane. Needless to say, we felt a little uncomfortable with all the Bibles and Hebrew material still in our possession. We began to take a severe dislike to the KGB and the Soviet "system".

Our suitcase of "important documents" was ever-present. We prayed to know exactly what to do with the contents. Always we were tailed by the KGB and soon we were able to identify them in the crowds of people around us while shopping or sightseeing. By the time we arrived in Moscow, we knew we had to make our move to distribute the Bibles and Hebrew teaching materials. We decided to take them to the synagogue but first to lose our tails as we didn't intend to jeopardize the recipients. While touring Moscow, three couples in our group got off the tour bus in the middle of town. One couple went by taxi to the Baptist church while another couple went by another taxi to the synagogue with the suitcase. Meridel and I went shopping to draw the tails in our direction. We waited several hours and then headed back to our hotel. By this time it was almost dark and we were eager to hear how the synagogue contact had turned out. We couldn't talk in the hotel so we had to go for a walk to discuss the details. They told us that the old Rabbi was overwhelmed by sight of the bibles and primary Hebrew readers. When he opened the suitcase and saw its contents, without a word he fell on his knees weeping and kissed the hands of the donors.Some say that it was foolish to take them to the synagogue because of Communist party infiltrators, but the response of the old Rabbi dispelled our fears.

A Word of Release

The next day we were touring the Kremlin, the walled section of Old Moscow. It was actually a fortification build over the centuries to protect the Czars from enemy attacks. It is the virtual seat of Soviet power. The high walls and ubiquitious golden domes spires with crosses on top recall the original purpose for the area and the historic connections of Church and State. Our guide pointed out the administration buildings and congress halls and said, "This is where the Party Secretary and Premier, Mr. Brezhnev have their offices." This was our cue. Several people slipped away from the main group and hand-delivered our letter and petition to Mr.Brezhnev's office. It was promised that the letter would be personally delivered. That night we had extra KGB guards assigned to us and they even tried to trick us by having a young girl who spoke good English telephone our hotel room. She said very sweetly, "Mrs Rawlings, the underground church and I hope you have some Bibles for us". Meridel immediately knew this was a trap and just as sweetly replied, "My dear, you are entirely mistaken".

On the following evening, our last in Russia at that time, a small group of us gathered in front of Lenin's Tomb. Other tourists were there to see the changing of the guard. We drew aside from the main body of spectators and began to pray. Together we agreed for the release of Soviet Jewry and restated, by faith, those ancient prophetic words, **"I will say to the North, 'Give Up' "**.[1] The bitter Siberian wind blew the words back into our faces and we felt very insignificant. The Soviet darkness seemed to envelop us naturally and spiritually. We hurried back to the warmth of our hotel rooms to pack. The following morning we left Moscow's International airport. It was still dark at 7 a.m. We felt pain at leaving our Russian Jewish friends behind, but happy that we had obeyed the Lord. Little did we realize the surprise that waited for us in Jerusalem a few days later.

Our Aeroflot flight landed us in Cyprus. Immediately a feeling of joy, relief and freedom

[1] *Isaiah 43:6*

welcomed us in Nicosia as we relaxed in the Mediterranean sunshine and balmy temperatures.

Several days later we arrived in Jerusalem. As soon as we got into our hotel room, I went down to the lobby and bought a Jerusalem Post. To my astonishment, the headlines read, "Kremlin agrees to release 300,000 Soviet Jews over next decade". I hurried to tell Meridel. "Look" I said, "God has answered our prayers". We both eagerly read the articles and shared it with the others in our tour group. It was not just coincidence that we had been in the Soviet Union exactly on the days when the Kremlin decision to release Soviet Jews was being made. Speaking that word of release now made sense. We asked forgiveness for our unbelief.

Opening Gates

One of the key factors in the Kremlin decision was economics. The Soviets had wanted for years more open trade agreements with the USA. A Bill was debated in the American Senate and House of Representatives regarding trade with the USSR. Senator Henry Jackson penned his famous amendment to the bill and it passed, linking Soviet emigration policy and trade credits with the USA. Senator Jackson, long a champion for the cause of Soviet Jewry, finally put teeth in the issue and the Soviets backed down because of their perilous economic condition. They needed American trade and technology in exchange for emigration of Jews.

Over the next twelve years some 270,000 Jews left the Soviet Union. The peak year was in 1979 when more than 51,000 were given exit visas. Since that time with the passing of Brezhnev and Andropov the number of exit visas given annually has dropped off sharply until in 1984 only some 896 were released.

Once again the gates out of the Soviet Union have been shut. A new era of Soviet propaganda has arisen, this time singling out the Zionists as the enemies of the Soviet people. Ancient spirits of anti-semitism have arisen from their graves, dressed in new anti-Zionist terminology. The appalling post-Andropov era singled out the Jews who requested to go to Israel. It has signalled a Stalinist revival. Never before has action on behalf of Soviet Jewry been more appropriate or needed.

During the years from 1972 to 1982 Meridel, the boys and I were very busy. We travelled nearly continuously, staying in some places a day, others a week, some a month and even in a few places a year or more. We covered the globe looking for Jewish people to share with them the promises for the Torah and Tanach[1] concerning their responsibility to return to Israel.

After our trip to Russia and Israel in 1972 we returned to the U.S.A. for several months. At once the local Jewish community was astonished by the fact that Christians would visit their people behind the Iron Curtain. They were touched by our sincerity. I shared a planned visit to South America. They were pleased and asked us to help awaken their Latin American communities to the need of action on behalf of Soviet Jewry. We were glad to oblige and the heads of the local Jewish Federation in Richmond Virginia gave us letters of endorsement to the various communities

[1] *Torah and Tanach: Hebrew reference to the Old Testament.*

throughout South America.

From 1972 to 1976 Meridel, the boys and I visited ninty-five countries on behalf of Israel and the Jews in Soviet Union. We visited every country in South America, some more than once, singling out the Jewish communities and their leaders. In each place we had unique experiences. The Jews thought for sure that we were missionaries and the Christians thought we were purveyors of some strange doctrine. Everyone kept us at arm's length. However, the letters of endorsement given by the Jewish community in the Unites States really did help to break down the barriers with the South American communities. Many of those experiences are recorded in "Fishers and Hunters".

By and large, not much had been done by the Latin American Jewish Communities on behalf of Soviet Jewry. Most of the people were very affluent and they generally weren't too interested in the plight of their brothers in Russia nor in considering making "aliyah"[1] to Israel. However, we persevered.

In the early mid-seventies, numerous committees and Jewish action groups on behalf of Soviet Jewry were formed world-wide. Written articles and books including "The Jews of Silence" by Elie Wiesel served to generate interest and concern among Jews, especially in France, USA, Great Britain and Australia. However, South American Jewry was quite uninvolved in the cause and our visits there hopefully stimulated some response.

[1] "Aliyah": *"To go up" generally used in reference to go up to Zion.*

Closing Gates

With interest we all watched the Soviet relaxation of the Diploma Tax[1] on Jews and the increased numbers of exit visas granted during the 1970's. By 1979 the exodus peaked with 51,320 exit visas granted to Jewish applicants. Through the late '70's, however, a trend began to develop that caused the Soviets to close the gates. Despite several warnings from Moscow an increasing number of Soviet emigrees "dropped out" of going to Israel once they arrived in transit stations in Vienna and Rome. In the early seventies, nearly 95% of all emigrants came to Israel. However, soon greater and greater numbers of applicants for visas were not motivated by Zionist ideals and used the opportunity to escape Russia for the West with its attendant economic advantages. We are not going to debate the philosophy of "freedom of choice" offered to the Jews leaving the Soviet Union. This is an issue outside of the scope of this book, but I do feel that it is important to always tell the truth. The Russian Jews were permited to leave the Soviet Union on the understanding that they were going to Israel to be reunited with their families. In this regard it seems logical that all emigrants should have had at least enough courtesy to fulfil that obligation by going to Israel where their invitations originated. Then they have the opportunity to make their decision as to where they would like to live with their respective families. I say this in spite of

[1] Diploma Tax – *this was a tax levied on every Jew who was given permission to leave the U.S.S.R. The emigrants were obliged to pay the Soviet authorities the cost of their education. For university graduates, of which there were many, this could range from $15,000 to $25,000 or more, depending on the degree obtained.*

the fact I believe the Bible says that Jews should live in Israel, for the time of the Diaspora is closing with the creation of the State of Israel. As Dr. Abe Harman, the Chancellor of the Hebrew University in Jerusalem says, "The fact is, there is no exodus from the USSR without our soverign Jewish state to issue invitations".[1] Nevertheless, the statistics show that in 1973 the drop out-rate of Jews not going to Israel was 4.2%. This continued to grow to 49% in 1976, 66% in 1979 and 80% in 1981.

The Soviet response to this was to reduce the quota more and more. In 1984 the number of Jews who left the Soviet Union was 896, the lowest level since 1970. These figures were quoted in a joint statement in January 1985 by the National Conference on Soviet Jewry and the Greater New York Conference on Soviet Jewry. They said that these figures suggest that Moscow has effectively closed the gates on Jewish emigration.

The closure indicates that the Soviet Union has violated the Helsinki Accord. The USSR was a co-signer with twenty-five other nations of the 1975 Helsinki Accord which declares "That the participating States will respect human rights and fundamental freedoms, including the freedom of thought, conscience, religion or belief . . . " It also states, "every citizen has the right to leave any country including his own, and return to his country, and also that citizens have the basic right to become reunited with their families living in other countries."

The Soviet Union has consistently violated its international agreements including the UN Charter of Human Rights, ratified by the U.S.S.R. in 1962 as well as the Helsinki Accord and the Madrid

[1] *From a lecture at the Hebrew University of February 14, 1985.*

Accords in 1983. The Soviets hotly deny their culpability since their concessions are made on their own terms and understandings. They are, in fact, a law unto themsleves.

A final reason why the Soviet Government was hesitant to continue to grant special emigration privileges to the Jews was because they didn't want to set a precedent that would necessitate concessions being made to other national minority groups within the USSR effecting further internal de-stabilization. In the early '70's the Soviet regime was forced to make immigration concessions in order to obtain economic favours, but by the 1980's the conditions had changed such that a new purge of the "Zionists" was introduced that shut the gates with force. A new offensive from the free world was required.

4

The Battle Plan

"Speak up for those who cannot speak for themselves, for the rights of all those who are destitute.

Speak up and judge fairly. Defend the rights of the poor and needy"

Proverbs 31:8-9

Film Concept

Our 1983 Passover trip to the USSR had a profound effect on me personally and, as a result of meeting the courageous refuseniks in Kiev, Moscow and Leningrad, I was challenged to make a film on their behalf, giving them a voice to the free world. We came back to Israel in April 1983 and I couldn't stop thinking about Lev, Inna, and Carmi and the many others we had met. I knew I had to keep the word I had given to them when we departed. I would do my best to help them. I also knew how expensive it would be to produce a high-quality documentary on their plight; and in order to make a documentary that would have impetus and credibility we would have to have fresh material from inside Russia. I wanted the courage and the valiant spirit of my refusenik friends to be seen on film. I also knew that I would have to keep the project quiet. It was almost a contradiction of terms. On the one hand we needed support and help by many people to complete such a project. On the other hand we couldn't advertise our plans publicly for fear that the Soviets wouldn't grant us re-entry visas. It was almost a "Catch 22" situation.

In early June 1983 we went to North America for a three-month speaking tour. We showed slides of our trip the previous April which graphically portrayed the Elberts the day before Lev was summoned to KGB headquarters. By the time we began to speak out for him Lev was a "Prisoner of Zion". We asked people everywhere in churches, synagogues, community centres, on radio and television, to please send letters and telegrams protesting about Lev's horrible treatment. Throughout this time we could not mention publicly our plan to go back in and make a film. In mid-June I spoke to Bruce and Moira Allen in Toronto about the project. They were very moved by the needs of the refuseniks and agreed to help me make the film on their behalf.

Our itinerary took us all over North America and two of the many evenings that we participated in were held in Toronto and Boston. In Toronto representatives of the Conservative and Orthodox communities invited us to speak to the largest synagogue in North America – Beth Tzedek – on their "Mordecai Outcry" night on behalf of Soviet Jewry.

While in Boston we were interviewed by the CBS television news team on the steps of the State Capital building. We were guest speakers and participated in a candle-lit demonstration march through the city on behalf of Soviet Jewry. The event was arranged by the New England Christian Embassy Director Sandy O'Connel, and co-sponsored by Jewish community leaders. The theme of the evening was "The Gates are Closing".

We monitored the situation daily. People everywhere responded and sent telegrams to Lev. Inna began her first hunger strike or fast on August 1 1983. In a letter from Michael, Lev's brother, sent to Israel, he said, "You cannot imagine the strength of her indignation which gave her power not to take any food for 10 days and at the same time to run around from office to office in the General Prosecutor's building. It was a miracle she kept going".

Then on August 11 the authorities promised her letters from Lev and said that her complaints would be delivered to Yuri Andropov. Both promises were fulfilled and she broke the hunger strike. She then travelled to Moscow to continue her struggle for Lev in the highest offices of the USSR in the hope of convincing them that her husband was a victim of deliberate provocation. On August 14 an unknown woman called at the Elbert's home claiming to be the mother of one of Lev's fellow prisoners with a message from Lev that a search was going to be made of their flat and that the Elberts should get rid of any drugs on the premises. Haim Elbert, Lev's father, who spoke to this woman in Inna's absence noticed that this strange woman was driven off in a car commonly used by the KGB.

On August 26 when Inna returned to Kiev her apartment was searched by two police officers and an 'sniffer' dog. The dog found nothing and was taken away. Thirty minutes later the two policemen returned and searched again. This time they claimed to have found an envelope containing a brown powder which they considered to be a narcotic. Carmi then drew attention to the fact that the latch on their front door appeared to have been tampered with during her absence. Inna resumed her hunger strike the following day and once more departed to Moscow to protest over this latest 'frame up' and defamation tactic of the Kiev KGB.

On September 29, because of the critical state of her health after more than one month on a hunger strike, the Chief Rabbi of Israel, Rav Avraham Shapiro, sent Inna a telegram with his blessings and urgent demand for her to stop her hunger strike. This request could not be ignored since according to Rabbinic teaching it is "forbidden to endanger a soul". Inna thanked him for the care but answered that her fasting was her only weapon in the struggle for the life and freedom of her husband. Nevertheless, the authority of the Chief Rabbi combined with the telephone call of Rabbi Drukman also from Israel, and with the insistent demands of her close friends and physicians convinced her to stop her hunger strike on October 5 after 37 days!

Haim Elbert summed up the situation on October 11 when he said in a letter to Israel: "This investigation procedure and blatant frame-up of my son has taken the Soviet regime back to the days of Stalin and Beria".

Due to Inna's persistence and fastings, during this time Lev was able to send the following letters from prison to her and to friends in the West:

September,1983

"Dear . . . .

Thank you for your letters. They are my hope. Unfortunately I am not in a position to celebrate our holidays in a proper way. More than that I have to eat food not prepared according to our laws. I hope that the Lord will not judge me too severely because He said in the Scriptures, 'I gave you this law to live according to it'. To live and not to die . . .

I was happy to receive your letter. I was particularly delighted to see the picture of the Mount of the Temple and of the summer garden. Yes, Leningrad is beautiful.[1]

I am a conservative person and therefore try to answer accurately all letters I receive. Of course sometimes the letters are delayed or even lost, but it is one of the inexplicable peculiarities which characterizes my correspondence. I hope that the Lord will keep you to the last moment and 'bear you up on eagles wings' which is written in the book of Isaiah.

Shalom.

August, 1983

"Dear . . . .

. . . I would like to send you my Rosh Hashanna greeting and to wish that your family be written into the Book of Life . . .

I am okay, daily working to fulfill my quota.[2]

I am making string bags for agricultural

[1] *He has received a picture of the Temple Mount in Jerusalem but it was described as a summer garden in Leningrad to get by the postal censors.*

[2] *Not to fulfill a daily quota is a serious breach of the rules in the labour camp and brings severe punishment.*

production. The attitude toward me is good now.[1]

"Dear October,1983

I celebrated the Holy Days[2] in my memory. In my mind I was shaking a lulav and etrog[3]. In my mind I was going around the synagogue with the Torah Scroll on Ha shannah Raba and dancing with it in my arms on Simchat Torah.

My affairs are going according to my recent talk with the investigator for the Kiev Prosecutor's Office. It seems that in the very near future I will be permitted to receive letters and answer them only twice a month. So it threatens to make our correspondence one-sided. Nevertheless, I believe that everything will be all right because I totally trust in his leading hand, not failing however to try to help myself with my human hands . . .

Shalom,

Lev.

Carmi Elbert, now 13, grew up a refusenik child and witnessed the terrible provocation and harassment of his parents. Early in 1984 Carmi was threatened at school. If he didn't comply with the demands of the Communist Youth League, he was told that his family history of anti-Soviet activity would be revealed to his classmates. In spite of intense peer pressure Carmi bravely stood by his parents and their desire to go to Israel. It was then

[1] *The fact that many letters had been sent to Lev from the USA and Canada augered well for Lev. He also received letters from his family and friends in the USSR. The authorities take this very seriously and it can serve to reduce the harsh attitudes of guards and prison officials.*

[2] *Rosh Hashanna, the Jewish New Year, and the Feast of Tabernacles or Succot.*

[3] 'Lulav' *is a special heart of a palm and* 'etrog' *is a type of citrus fruit placed inside the succah or tabernacle build only at Succot to remind the Jewish people of God's presence and provision in the wilderness.*

that the die was cast and Carmi became the scapegoat for the KGB pressure put on the children of refuseniks. The savage beating that he received was premeditated and engineered by the authorities. To this day Carmi Elbert still suffers from the residual effects of blows to the head by an iron bar and kicks sustained on his back and kidneys.

It is gratifying to note that because the Elberts stood fast in their convictions and Western pressure was applied, Lev's increased sentence of three years based on the frame-up was mysteriously removed and he was released from the labour camp in June 1984, after serving one year.

In September 1983, we finished our North American speaking tour in Toronto. There our friends Jacques and Rani Gauthier had arranged a 'film fund raiser' for us. Jacques is a successful young lawyer who has specialized in International Law. Having studied in Montreal and in Geneva and fluently bilingual in French and English, his legal council is earnestly sought. Several years ago he and his beautiful wife met the Living God. As committed Christians they have taken on the challenge of Jesus to "love one's neighbour as thyself", which they do in practical ways. In the midst of Jacques' busy law practice he succeeded in arranging a luncheon of interested friends from the Toronto area. This began the seven-phase plan that was aimed at completing the film. We were ably assisted in financial matters by our friend of university days Grant Bartlett. Prayer support came from Rev.Clyde Williamson, Chairman of the Canadian Friends of the International Christian

Embassy and Assistant Pastor at Queensway Cathedral in Toronto. We incorporated our non-profit film project. The title **'Gates of Brass'** was chosen some months later.

The following phases represent the basic steps in the production of **Gates of Brass**:

Phase 1 Preliminary funding for the Russia trip and film.
Phase 2 Trip to Russia with film crew to obtain interviews with refuseniks.
Phase 3 Production of a 5-minute film clip from Russian interviews on 16mm film.
Phase 4 Use of clip to raise funds to cover remaining cost of principle photography.
Phase 5 Filming in Israel, England, and USA. Interviews and dramatic sequences.
Phase 6 Post production, editing of film and collection of stock footage; simultaneous fund-raising for remainder of film.
Phase 7 Release of film with various premiers throughout the world.
Phase 8 Distribution of film worldwide.

Phase 1 – Preliminary Funding

The production of any motion picture, whether documentary or dramatic, in 16mm or 35mm format is a long and arduous task. It involves the skills of many people, much equipment, and in our case various travel expenses. Often people ask me why it costs so much to make a film. My answer is simply to ask them in return how much would it cost to make 1,290,000 photographs? This is approximately how many individual pictures are taken to make a one hour film. This is calculated on the basis of 24 frames per second with a 15-to-1 ratio. That is, 24 pictures are shot every second the camera is running; and in a one hour docu-drama it is estimated that approximately 10-15 times more film is shot than is used to ensure the best results possible after editing. Then of course there are labour costs for the hundreds of man-hours required of various skills such as cameramen, sound technicians, lighting experts, location managers, grips, script writers, narrator; plus of course music producers, the film producer and director. In addition heavy expenses are involved in the rental of laboratory facilities and special technical equipment. The breakdown of costs involves three main divisions: film and equipment, labour, and production costs.

In our production **Gates of Brass** we also needed preliminary funding for costs involved in raising the money to go into the Soviet Union. We had decided that the production depended heavily on getting the best possible interviews with refuseniks inside Russia. This was imperative to make the production unique and newsworthy. Therefore we broke the production down into phases. We said that if we were able to shoot the footage in Russia then get it out with all the KGB surveillance,this would be a miracle and would indicate that we should proceed to the next phase.

Phase 2 – Trip to Russia

From June 1983 secret plans were made to enter the USSR in late October of that year. As producers, Meridel and I were to accompany the film crew. This film was our vision and we were experienced in making contact with the refuseniks. All plans were finalized and many people gave sacrificially to help us purchase our tickets and equipment. Others prayed and fasted for us. We planned to meet the film crew in Switzerland for several days of prayer and detailed preparation.

Early in October we were busy in Jerusalem with many activities when suddenly Meridel began to feel ill. We knew she was expecting a baby and were thrilled as we had hoped and prayed for another child for six years. On October 4th the obstetrician tried to find the baby's heart beat but was unsuccessful. He then suggested an ultrasound scan. This was accomplished and the baby was diagnosed as approximately 14 weeks. Then, a week later, the doctor broke the news that the baby had died and that Meridel must stay in hospital until the baby could be delivered. We asked the doctor if she could go on the trip to Russia in two weeks. He assured us that she would be all right to travel. Then began a nightmare experience as the medical procedure prescribed for Meridel failed repeatedly.

Never before have I felt so helpless. Meridel was undergoing excruciatingly painful labour induced by drugs, yet her body failed to respond. The day before we were to leave for the Soviet Union there was still no change and Meridel's life was hanging in the balance. I went to visit her in the hospital. I prayed before I went and I was completely convinced I should scrap the trip as she was my most important responsibility. We prayed together at her bedside and she looked so tired, pale and weak.

I said, "Darling, I am going to cancel the trip . . ."

But before I could finish the sentence she said weakly, "Wait, I have asked the Lord. I know you should go and when you do He will take care of me".

In sorrow I left Israel for Europe on my way to Russia. I knew that Meridel was in the Lord's hands, but the separation was really hard to sustain since her condition was not yet resolved. The loss of our baby and Meridel's suffering dragged out for almost a full month and is part of the price we paid for the production of this film.

Our child was a boy whom we named Victor. Attendants at the Share Tzadek (Gates of Righteousness) Hospital comforted Meridel by telling her that he would be buried in Jerusalem and not thrown into an incinerator as is the general practice in many hospitals around the world. This sorrow served to help us identify with the pain and anguish of Soviet Jews separated from family and loved ones.

The crew and I made our European rendezvous in the home of Hans Jorge and Astrid Bishof, the Swiss Director of the International Christian Embassy Jerusalem. Their kindness and hospitality really touched our hearts. I was in constant telephone contact with Meridel up until the very moment we boarded the flight to Moscow with still no change in her condition. My concern was now increased as from here on I had no possibility of contacting her from Russia.

At this juncture it is extremely important to point out that countless people were praying and interceding for us all through this time. We really thank God for each one who stood with us in this way. An example of the power of intercessory prayer is found at the end of this chapter.

Before our arrival at the International Airport in Moscow we had decided that I would do all the reconnaissance work in the U.S.S.R alone while the film crew would remain quiet in their hotel and pray. We were whisked through the passport and customs checks and arrived in our hotel tired and hungry. All the restaurants were closed.

That night I decided to make contact with my refusenik friends who we had visited the previous April. By memory I sought my way on public transport. I didn't take taxis in front of the hotel as they often had KGB connections. Searching around I finally found the home of our friends. Upon arrival at their door, I gave a gentle knock. The KGB always knock hard or ring the buzzer. The noises inside were immediately silenced. The door was opened only a crack by my friend's wife who asked in Russian, "Who is it?"

"It's Jay, remember me? I was here at Pessach", I whispered.

"My God", she exclaimed. As she threw open the door she gave me a great big hug. "You are the first visitor to come to us since the downing of the Korean jet liner".

I entered and after whispered greetings to all the family I began to write out on paper all my news. We sat around the small kitchen table. As soon as I had written my plans they were read and immediately burned in a large tin can that sat in the middle of the table. All evidence of our silent communication was promptly destroyed. This was done so that any listening devices in the room would not pick up our conversation.

We agreed that they would arrange the time and

date of a rendezvous for the filming and that I would come back the following day to get the details. I returned to the hotel late my first night in Moscow tired, but filled with a sense of having begun to accomplish that which was heavy on my heart.

The next day we began the sightseeing routine. That night I returned to the home of my friend and they had everything set for the following morning at another location. Also at their apartment that night was Alexander Yudborovsky from Leningrad who just 'happened' to be visiting in Moscow. The timing of his visit was absolutely miraculous for I could not make advance arrangements with my refusenik friends in Leningrad via public telephone. As a result, we were able to arrange beforehand our filming in Leningrad. We set the time and the place.

The following morning I led the film crew, flight bags of camera equipment in hand, to our Moscow location. It was a cold, grey November day. We found the apartment block easily but finding the actual film site was more difficult. Finally we entered and, as I had previously arranged, no English was spoken. This was done so that anyone listening could not tell that there were foreigners present. I wrote out every question in English which was translated into Russian orally.

Before we started I asked the refuseniks if they would prefer me not to film them, or to film them in such a way as to conceal their identity. I felt it was important to give them this option since their participation could cost them dearly in KGB harassment and/or prison sentences. Anatoly Scharansky was put in jail for 13 years on a charge of 'treason'. This courageous young man, with his infectious enthusiasm and sense of humour was interviewed in a car and in a Moscow park by British television. Shortly after the program was released in the West, he was put into jail on trumped-up charges. All the force of the Soviet 'legal' system was thrown against him. He was used as an example to scare other Jews from speaking the truth.

We are painfully aware of his tragic history so I asked the refuseniks if they would like me to pack up the cameras and go home. Their answers astounded me. They said, **"If we don't speak up now the KGB has us in the place they want us! We don't want to hide our faces."**

The camera was carefully wrapped to insulate the sound of the drive motor and film passing through the shutter. In order to accomplish this Bruce, as the cameraman, was completely wrapped up in a quilt designed for the severest Siberian winter. After every interview he would emerge in a sea of perspiration. Each Russian refusenik was perfect on camera, succinct and to the point.

We had the camera and microphone set up in one room and while we were filming, the others waited in the adjacent living-room in silence. Every so often the sun would break through the clouds outside giving an illustration of the bright hopes behind the blackness of life as a refusenik. Each person spoke about various aspects of their lives as refuseniks, and never once did they attack the Soviet Union. Their struggle is not against the Communist system. All they desire to do is to leave and to be reunited with their families in Israel.

Upon the completion of this hair-raising work, we thanked each one for their comments and then we took turns exiting one by one into the street. Carefully, yet nonchalantly, we made our way back to the centre of Moscow and resumed our activities as tourists.

Our next destination was Leningrad. Upon arrival, in spite of a heavy downpour, thousands of workers were outside putting up massive signs – red and black murals with Marxist slogans – in preparation for the annual "1917 Revolution Day Celebrations" in this, the city of its beginning.

Eleven years had passed since on the same day in Moscow's Red Square we had stood by faith and proclaimed the eternal words, **"I will say to the North 'give up'** and **'let my people go' "**.

Our Leningrad touring schedule was prepared by the Russian Intourist officials in our hotel. Carefully we planned to clandestinely visit our refusenik friends. On our second day in Leningrad and under the cover of night, we travelled by bus to the end of the line and descended into the blackness. We glanced in each direction – no tails.

Quickly we walked through a grove of silver birch trees standing like sentinels, their bare branches casting long shadows at our feet. We made our way along the frozen street, found the apartment, mounted the old rickety staircase, and knocked gently at the door. We waited.

Slowly the door opened and we were greeted by Eugenia Utevskaya and her husband, Alexander Yudborofsky, whom I had met previously in Moscow. Their careful smiles reassured us. They took our coats and we entered their living-room. It was crowded with refuseniks and dimly lit. One central light bulb hung from the ceiling. All eyes fixed on us. At first there was an awkward silence: Then I shook hands with each one and took paper and wrote what I intended to do. Again I wrote to avoid the ears of the KGB listening devices commonly placed in dwellings where the agents were suspicious of the occupants.

I explained that we had come to Russia to help the refuseniks and to give them a voice in the world. The way I proposed to do this was by means of a documentary film. Again I was amazed at their positive response. They eagerly wanted to know more. As in Moscow, we all knew that their participation is such a film could land them in jail. I wrote that we hadn't come to make their lives more difficult; and we said that if they were in any way hesitant to make statements on film or on tape we would simply pack up our equipment and go back to the West with our admiration unchanged. Their answer was unanimous. They said, **"If we don't speak now, then the KGB have already beaten us with their terror tactics. Of course we will speak!"** Loud and clear their voices rang out,describing that they were not against the Soviet Union but that they simply wanted to have the right to go to their biblical homeland, Israel.

When we had finished the interviews we all decided that it was better to move outside into the darkness and away from hidden microphones. We found a forest glen near the apartment building. Huddling together we had a strong sense of oneness; and my Jewish friends began to share their hopes, anxieties and aspirations with me. Their courage to speak the truth in the very jaws of the "Russian Bear" was challenging and inspiring.

With arms locked together I told them everything that was on my heart to try and do for them. We spent about 15 minutes communicating like this. We lingered a few more moments painfully aware of the possibility that this would be our only meeting.

We returned from Leningrad to Moscow to finalize our secret arrangements to have the film placed in safe-keeping. Some months later, the film was brought out to the West by a secret courier. For obvious reasons we cannot go into details about this arrangement.

On the day of our departure we were all quite anxious to leave. We had hours to wait before the Intourist car would come to pick us up to take us to the airport. Three hours before our departure an impressive black limousine appeared at the hotel for us. We thought it strange. Outside the weather had turned bitterly cold, with a severe wind that brought rain, sleet, snow, thunder and lightning all at once. It was a wild storm; and I wondered if the plane would be delayed because of the weather.

While we drove to the airport something very odd began to happen. We were in the middle of a storm; but far off in the distance, almost on the horizon, the sun was shining brightly with golden rays shooting to the ground.

I felt sure it was like a sign to us. It was! We were truly in a storm for upon arrival at the airport area, immediately a porter was there to help us with our bags. We were hurried along to the customs area before stopping at the check-in counter.

We were taken aside from the other people checking in and then it all happened. Slowly but calculatingly a wave of KGB officers in plainclothes began to open our suitcases and to search our belongings. They knew we had something and they were going after it. Once they had opened all our luggage, including the camera equipment, they began to photograph us. First they took still photos, then video recordings. We instantly became famous in the USSR. They x-rayed every item in our suitcases, even our batteries. Then they began to single me out; and when I demanded why we were being detained and searched, the highest ranking officer, a thin, older man in a grey suit, stepped up and in a gruff manner said, "You've been visiting refusers. You have anti-Soviet material!"

He picked up our film and handed it to another man and he exited through a door with it. I demanded that it be brought back immediately as it was private property and that they had no right to take my film. He smiled coldly and in a slow, sinister way produced a paper written in Russian.

"Here, sign this, and put your name and address here. After we have examined your film and proven that it is not anti-Soviet material, we will return it to you".

I recognized that this was a ploy to get me to sign my own admission of guilt for their records and the possible implication of our Jewish friends. Instead of providing them the satisfaction of my giving in, I refused. Then I demanded that I have access to my Canadian Embassy for help.

However I knew that this was futile. Surrounded by hostility I remembered a premonition I had before leaving Israel. I recalled my telephone conversation with the First Secretary of our Canadian Embassy in Tel Aviv.

I told him of my plans to film refuseniks in Russia and could I expect any help from our Embassy in Moscow should I get caught? He said he would find out for me. Coded telexes were sent to Moscow via Ottowa and the answer came back from our Embassy: " If you are apprehended, don't call on us!".

The KGB men continued to smile smugly in response to my obvious helplessness. Moira was in tears by this time and the plane was ready to leave. The KGB insisted that we get on the flight without our film. We were angry and frustrated, and helpless.

We were experiencing first-hand something of the iron rule of this Soviet system. Again I refused to sign the paper and demanded heatedly, "Why are you so threatening?" At that the KGB chief said sternly, "You seem to forget that we are at war!".

There was nothing left to do but go aboard the waiting plane. You can well imagine the heaviness of our hearts, the guilt and dread that filled our thinking, because now that part of the film was lost, we knew that we had put our precious friends in jeopardy. We still couldn't bring our minds to think of the back-up plan that had been previously prepared if were were caught.

Strong forces of frustration, anger, and self-condemnation hung over all of us at failing to get our film out on the first try. Painfully we boarded our flight to Frankfurt, and despite the delicious food and the pleasant flight towards freedom I couldn't eat a bite. We were devastated by our battle with the forces of darkness.

I called Meridel upon arrival in Germany and found out the hell she had been through. I was, however, greatly relieved to know that she was over the worst and slowly recovering. I shared our ordeal with the KGB, the confiscated film, and the duplicate of the film in safe-keeping in Moscow. I asked her to relay the message to a friend in Jerusalem, who in turn would pass the message on to our friends in Moscow, telling them what had happened in a veiled way. All of our concern was for the precious people in Moscow and Leningrad who we had interviewed.

In several days I returned home to Jerusalem after saying farewell to our film crew who had performed so well under pressure. Thus began two long months of waiting for news of the film from Russia. I was in constant touch with my courier by telephone. He kept telling me to be patient. Finally the countdown began. He personally arranged for the internal transfer. The film was on its way out.

He gave me specific instructions as to when and where to pick it up in Europe. I quickly arranged my departure from Israel. Then I waited it out in Europe at our rendezvous airport. The day it was supposed to appear nothing showed up. I impatiently waited out two more days. My charter flight for New York was scheduled to leave the next day and I had to make the contact or forfeit my ticket. The person who was meeting me at the airport didn't know me, so I had to stand with a placard with his name written on it. Flight after flight arrived with still no contact. Then at 4:30 p.m. in the afternoon he appeared. He motioned for me to come aside from the crowd of people. He spoke very little English. He opened his briefcase and quickly handed me a white package. I opened it on one end and there to my amazement were the films that had been hidden in Russia. I gave him a hug and he was gone. I went back to the hotel room and slept with the film under my pillow and mattress.

The following day I flew to North America. Since the film was exposed and sensitive to the x-ray machines that are found at every security check in airports, I had to literally wear it on my body. The pockets of my trench coat were stuffed and I'm sure I looked just like the 'Michelin man'.

Bruce and Moira were waiting for me at the airport in Canada. When I saw them in the arrival area, we greeted each other and then I felt two men take both my arms and escort me to a waiting car. Bruce didn't want to take any chances and had two of the Royal Canadian Mounted police friends escort us home. The following day we had the film developed in the presence of a uniformed policeman. The film came out perfectly. It was a miracle of the first order. We thanked God for the help He had given us to this point.

Phase 3 – Production of a 5-minute film clip

With the super-8 mm film from Russia now in the West, Bruce Allen then set about to take two interviews of the nine that we shot and to make them into a 5-minute film clip with English dubbed over the Russian. This served as our primary tool in raising the rest of the budget. These are the English translations of the statements made in Leningrad and Moscow by Leonid Kelbert and Yalena Dubianskaya, respectively.

Leonid is a film producer. He was born in 1945 and is married to a physician. They have two little girls. He has been a refusenik since 1978 and, in spite of repeated KGB harassment, has continued to encourage his people by creating a Jewish

Theatre. His play **Massada** has been seen by hundreds of Jews in the USSR.

'My name is Leonid Kelbert. I am a film director. I have been a refusenik for four years. Strictly speaking, I ceased to be a film director four years ago inasmuch as I was fired from work before I applied for a visa; and consequently I was no longer able to work in my field. I remained without work for a year and a half and then I managed to get a job in a more or less related profession. Nevertheless I am not disenchanted since life as a refusenik, despite all the complications and vicissitudes, turned out to be a much more significant, more important, more creative period of time for me then my entire life before that. We are happy that we found such an opportunity to become involved in the history, culture, and heritage of our people, something which we were previously unaware of. But nevertheless we continually feel how the situation changes, how the tension mounts, how time passes. And we want to say that no one knows whether we shall be able to address you in the future saying what we want to say.

Martin Buber once said that, " . . . Jews are a community of people based on a common historical memory". Yes. But our historical memory is full not only with great events, but also with sad ones. History is also being made today. We, on our part, are prepared to do our utmost to make history, but it doesn't depend only on us. Not only we make history, every Jew makes it, no matter where he lives, no matter where he is. And today, now, while we still can, we want to remind everyone of this – that our common history is made by our joined hands. And what we leave to our grandchildren and our descendents depends on us, on each of us today.

That is all. Thank you'.

Yalena Dubianskaya is a brilliant economist who lost her job when she and her husband Eric applied to go to Israel. Eric is a former metallurgical engineer and they have a daughter, Inna, who is 14.

'From the very moment when I sensed Israel within me, in my fate, I have had a sensation of unity and participation in the fate of my people. This is an extraordinary feeling of historical, cultural, and blood tie with one's people. I particularly sense this at the time of Jewish holidays, when I know that precisely at this moment millions of Jews are sensing and feeling the exact same thing as I am, are recalling their past and thinking about the future. And this sensation comes to me not only on holidays. I feel it daily, every minute; and my dream is that I should have this sensation, not only in spite of the circumstances in which I am living, that I should have it forever. But this could happen only if I would be together with my people, in my country, in my homeland, in Israel.

I have a feeling of unity, a feeling of belonging to everything that is connected to the Jewish people which is not only marvellous, it does not let me live calmly as long as there are people who are subjected to more difficult trials. I shall mention only two people whose tragic experiences are known to you; and the circumstances of these people does not let me live in peace. These are Felix Kochubievsky from Novosibirsk and Yury Tarnopolsky from Kharkov. I want to convey this, my sensation, to you. I want you to always remember these people, not to forget them. I want to tell you that we have a sensation of belonging, a sensation of unity and communality with one's people; and it will be transmitted to my daughter, too.

This is the goal and task of my life: to be together with my people, to help them, because only an equal member of each nation in this world can lead the nation toward progress. For me this is the main thing. This is the goal of my entire life. I want to say that the children of my children and the grandchildren of my grandchildren must live in Israel, and only then will they feel themselves full equal Jews. Only then will they be able to choose the way of life which they desire'.

Phase 4 – Use of film clip to raise funds.

During the spring months of 1984, I travelled throughout North America and Europe preparing an itinerary for the summer. Meridel and the boys and I would work together. We have been separated so much in the past as a family that we felt it imperative to travel together with our boys aged 10, 13, and 15. The finances for our sons' travel expenses came to us entirely separately from the film project.

Phase 5 – Filming the dramatic sequences.

Now that we had the film out of Russia and sufficient funds to proceed we began filming in earnest. Bruce and Moira Allen,very talented film makers from Canada, arrived in Jerusalem as our Director and his assistant. They have made over one hundred films and brought with them a special sensitivity to the project. We had worked closely together on **Apples of Gold** and were grateful for their input.

For the first few days we discussed the entire project. We decided the best way to begin was to concentrate on the violations of the principles of human rights by the Soviets, instead of on one or two high-profile individuals. This was done for a specific reason. One of the greatest limiting factors of any documentary film related to a historic scenario is that it dates itself very quickly. We wanted to avoid this if possible. So we decided to give an overall historic perspective by interviewing Jews who had left the Soviet Union at various stages over the last 30 years up to the present. Once we had a variety of interviews that gave illustrations of anti-Soviet activity leveled at the Jews, we could plan which scenes we wanted to recreate. Eventually we narrowed the field down to Carmi's brutal attack, the KGB breakup of a Hebrew class, the planting of drugs in order to trump up charges, a prison sequence and a forest scene.

Creating the dramatic sequences was very challenging. For one thing we had to obtain authentic Russian police and military uniforms. These we rented from a professional costume agency in London. We also had to find a cast of over 100 people to fill the various roles. It was amazing how many appropriate-looking people we found. We also had to find locations that looked like Russia for these sequences. In addition, all the equipment and props had to be prepared. We worked very hard, sometimes up to 20 hours a day, everyone giving 100%, and eventually all the footage was "in the can".

We can look back now and laugh! Meridel and Moira scoured the city for costumes. For Carmi's scene, they visited a tiny second-hand clothing depot on Jaffa Road and came away loaded down with old white shirts, black shoes and a pair of striped pyjamas to be used later in the apartment raid sequence. The smile of the Orthodox owner of this little shop let them know they had made his day. They even found old ties for plainclothes KGB to wear, and fossilized school bags.

The problem was where would we find prison uniforms? The Israeli Defence Forces weren't about to come to our rescue. Our son David helped in the search. One day after school we went inside Herod's Gate in the Old City of Jerusalem and found a good second-hand store run by a gentleman whose father was an Arab, his mother a Jewess, and he had spent most of his life in America. Dave got the brain-wave of buying lab coats. Well, we looked at them and decided that they would do only if we could dye them. Moira and Meridel then began the search for dye. They headed for Sahaladin Street in East Jerusalem, but there was no gray dye on this entire street of shops. One must understand that in Israel to buy dye you visit a hardware store. After a two-hour frantic search they found 18 capsules of the exact colour in a small hardware store on the other side of town. Meridel used our largest cooking pots and began dying the eight lab coats after they had been altered to the correct length.

The Carmi scene was fun. Bruce, Moira, and Meridel visited the Anglican School to find 'bullies' that looked somewhat Russian. Amit, a 13-year-old Israeli friend who often came to our home to ride

BMX bikes with the boys, volunteered to play Carmi.

The first step in preparing the bullies for their role was to have their long locks sheared off! They looked years younger with their closely shorn haircuts. The day scheduled for filming was foggy and very overcast. We worked outside in the street from 8:00 a.m. to 1:30 p.m. until we had finished the sequence. As we piled the boys into our VW van to drive them home, the heavens opened and down came the rain.

The scene must have looked authentic, for the local neighbours, older Sephardim (Eastern Jews) sat on the steps of adjoining buildings to watch. Israeli police guarded the street to keep the traffic away. One religious Jew, a Hassid, walking by stopped when he saw Amit with the fake blood dripping from his ear and mouth and wanted to rescue him. The police explained that we were only making a film.

Amit proved to have a most willing spirit, in spite of the fact he had to play the part of the victim of cruel anti-semitism. There is a lot more to this curly-headed Israeli than meets the eye. We hugged Amit when we dropped him off at his house. He had done a great job as Carmi.

I remembered an incident several months earlier when our son David was helping Amit with an English essay homework assignment entitled, "What does an Israeli boy think of?" I was intrigued, and although it was his bedtime I said, "Read it to me Dave". Here is the essence of what Amit had written.

'An Israeli boy thinks about his Dad when he is in Lebanon and wonders, "Will he come home?". An

Israeli boy thinks, "My brother is going into the Army soon. Will he survive?" An Israeli boy thinks that in a few years he will be in the Army, too. An Israeli boy thinks about dying!'

Robert Brass, our Jerusalem location manager, offered each of the policemen that guarded the road 5,000 sheckels (about $10.00 at that time) each for their efficiency on our behalf. One of them responded with, "Technically I can have you arrested for offering a policeman a bribe; but I'll let it slide for now". They both chuckled, but he did not take the tip.

Finding locations was also a challenge. Bruce, Moira and Bill Martin, our driver would rise before sun-up at 4:30 a.m. and drive over every conceivable road in the Judean Hills overlooking the city of Jerusalem. Meridel was delegated the responsibility of finding a prison! Where does one start? Well, she went straight over to the Police Headquarters compound located next the the Russian Orthodox Church. Much to her joy, instead of coming up with blanks, one of the gentlemen in charge listened to her request and said, "Oh, Mrs. Rawlings, whatever you need, we will do. I haven't seen **Apples of Gold** yet, but I will".

He made reference to a reception that Meridel and I had attended at the police compound some months earlier with Mayor Kollek when the "Terrorist Victims' Fund" from the **Apples of Gold** film donated financial gifts to citizens of Jerusalem who had found bombs. Also a large gift went to police 'sappers' who dismantle these deadly devices. He quickly moved from behind his desk and commanded, "Follow me!" Robert Brass looked at her in utter amazement and said, "This is a miracle".

We walked past the Russian Orthodox Church, with golden onion domes, its bells ringing loudly. Just one block behind this church sits a former British prison, complete with gallows, now turned into a museum. It looked like what we wanted but we'd need Bruce, the Artistic Director, to give the final okay. Meridel was excited. Returning to his office, this gentleman related the following story: 'A former refusenik was walking through the Russian Compound one day and when she sighted the face of a man there, she froze with fear. Immediately she went to the gate of the police station and made an appointment to see one of the men in charge. Sitting in the office of a high police official she began, "I've come from Russia not long ago and there I was under continual surveillance by the KGB. Sir," she said, looking pale and shaken, "just a few minutes ago, I **saw** one of the men who followed me" . Non-plussed the policeman pulled out a large file and said, "Could you identify this man?" "Yes", was her immediate reply. She poured over the book of faces and stopped, put her finger on a man's photo, and said, "This is him!" "Yes", responded the policeman, "We know he is here and are keeping an eye on him" '.

Our entire prison sequence was filmed in the shadow of the Russian Orthodox Church. We moved quickly and quietly. No uniforms were worn outside of the prison. You can see with known KGB agents around, we didn't want to attract undue attention!

The Hebrew meeting was filmed in a downtown apartment. Our friends who owned it lacked the many chairs needed for the scene. Undaunted our hostess, Esther, simply lifted the telephone and called downstairs to the PLO's political office requesting to borrow some of the chairs that they use for their meetings. The response on the other end of the line was "Are you Communists?" I don't know what Esther said, but the chairs were delivered and used in this sequence.

Where were we going to get the refugees for the forest scene? We attend the local Baptist Church at No.4 Narkiss Street for worship on a Saturday morning. We meet in what we call the "Tin Tabernacle" as our church building was burned down in 1982. The guilty party has yet to be found. We meet in a very, very modest building made of sheet metal, plywood and plastic. It serves us well for the time being.

Dr. Bob Lindsey, our pastor, was more than willing to let me announce our need for extras. Before I stood to speak, a young lady from Holland slipped an envelope into my hand. On the outside she had written, "For the film". Inside were thirty-one hundred guilder notes.[1] Then from that brief announcement came the most willing and appropriate refugees for the forest sequence. Meridel then accompanied the crew to London for 10 days of interviewing with experts on Russian refuseniks including Professor Martin Gilbert, Rev.Michael Bourdeaux, founder of Keston College, and Miss Marjorie Farquarson of Amnesty International.

Quiet Contributors

Finances for the project have always been a tremendous consideration. Meridel and I have had to carry the responsibility for meeting the budget. It meant that in one year alone I was away from

[1] *Equivalent to about $1000.00 U.S.*

home for nine months. The burden has been considerable as no large organization, Christian or Jewish, has offered any assistance. The Christian Embassy in Jerusalem gave us the privilege of speaking during the Feast of Tabernacles, thereby alerting Christians world-wide of this project. Gratefully, we must recognize the outstanding effort on behalf of Soviet Jewry by Christians everywhere. Funds began to come into the project from all over the world. Prayer support was given by hundreds of people who prayed and fasted for the entire operation. Special recognition must to to Rev. Ralph Rutledge and his staff at the Queensway Cathedral in Toronto who spearheaded the "Esther Fast" world-wide. The funds have come as donations from individuals the world over who gave sacrificially; the old-age pensioners, housewives, students, people in wheelchairs, widows. They put most of us to shame.

Also supportive were the "End-Time Handmaidens and Servants" led by Gwen and Jim Shaw and Pastor Eloyse Badgett and her "Christian Living Fellowship" in Denver, Colorado who gave more per capita than any other church. Thanks go to Lily Myss-Hansen, leader of the Soviet Jewry Action prayer group in the International Christian Embassy in Jerusalem. (See Appendix).

Also Christian businessman Gustav Scheller of Bournemouth, England gathered many Israel-loving Christians together to hear Meridel and I share the plight of the refuseniks, and they have been a source of continual encouragement to us ever since with their prayers and giving. One of the most unusual and powerful groups was the Intercessory Prayer Group in one of Rev.Charlotte

Baker's freshman classes at Fountain Gate Bible Institute near Dallas,Texas. She challenged the students to pray for us while we were in the USSR. Their prayers were exactly timed during our entire trip in the USSR and for Meridel in Jerusalem. The Fountain Gate congregation, led by Pastor Fuchsia Pickett also prayed and gave generously. We also remember Faans Klopper, head of the International Christian Embassy for South Africa and Manfred and Inga Hagler who have faithfully supported this project since its inception.

Mention needs to be made here of the individuals from many nations who have given sacrificially. Christians, sensitive to the needs of the Soviet Jews placed $3,000.00 in our pockets at one time. One young teacher had her apartment broken into but the thief failed to find her savings and she alone gave $700.00.

I'll never forget the day we went to the post office in Jerusalem and opened a letter addressed to us in European script. We did not recognize the name of the sender. The letter enclosed explained that a German lady living on a small windswept island between Hamburg and Copenhagen in the North Sea had heard us speak of the plight of Soviet Jews. She had just sent DM30,000 into the project. She explained that her father, a former Nazi sympathizer, had reconciled himself to the Lord before dying and also left her an inheritance. She in turn sent it on to our Canadian office. We were so surprised and appreciative, but didn't realize the importance of her generosity or the perfect timing of it until Jay made a call to our accountant in Canada the very same day with the good news.

First he was greeted on the other end of the line with "Jay, I'm sorry, just today I told the staff they they had to quit work on the film as we are out of funds . . ."

An expensive gold bracelet was placed in the offering basket in a church in Berlin. On another occasion Jay and I prayed for an elderly German grandmother who was very crippled with arthritis. She became so improved that in just a few days she was out walking in the fruit orchard with her daughter. In response to her deliverance from pain she gave her gold watch and bracelet specifically for the work of the film. It is important to note that her son and daughter were in complete agreement with this.

From Switzerland a dedicated Christian lady sent in a total of 13,000 francs which went into the film. She lives a devoted life of prayer and service and believed our project worthwhile.

While speaking throughout South Africa I shall never forget the night that a shy young woman approached me. She stood waiting for me to answer the questions of countless people and when everyone else left, she stepped forward and placed a diamond ring in my hand and said "I too love the Jewish people, and pray for them daily. My husband and I are called to work in the "homelands" here with the blacks. We have talked it over and have agreed that we want this ring to go into the project because we want a part of this work. It is my engagement ring, and I'll send you the certificate of value right away".

There are no words . . .

The young adult group of the Queensway Cathedral in Toronto decided that they also

Lev Elbert's Kiev apartment. Communication only by writing because of the KGB bugging devices.
Lev wrote "Give us a voice!"

Inna, Carmi and Lev Elbert, Kiev.

Friends! Carmi Elbert, Refusinik 12 yrs old and Chris Rawlings 12 yrs from Jerusalem.

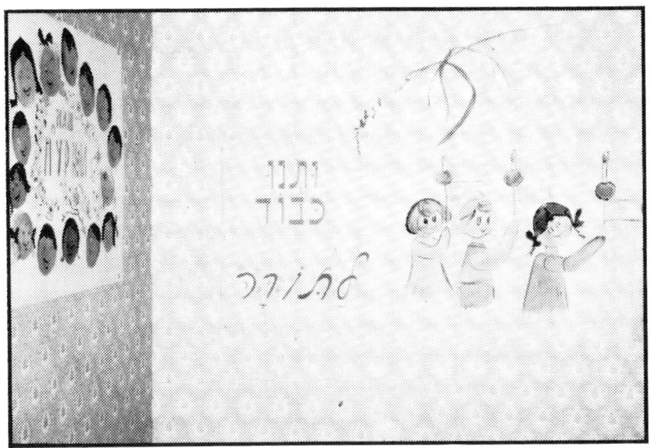

A handmade poster with Hebrew lettering in a Leningrad apartment.

This banner tells the story of Queen Esther's bravery on behalf of her people. The KGB stopped the celebration of Purim where the banner was to be used. Yaacov Rabinowitz (r) Jay Rawlings (l)

Long-term refuseniks Yalena Dubianskaya with her husband Eric in a Moscow Park

Ida Milgrom (l) mother of Leonid Shcharansky (r) anxiously waiting for the release of Anatoly from prison.

Photo by Juliene Paige

Isolde (l) & Vladimir (r) Tufeld in Moscow. Ailing parents of Igor Tufeld, interviewed for **Gates of Brass** in Jerusalem. Puppets are for teaching children of Jewish culture – a dream not yet fulfilled.

Photo by Juliene Paige

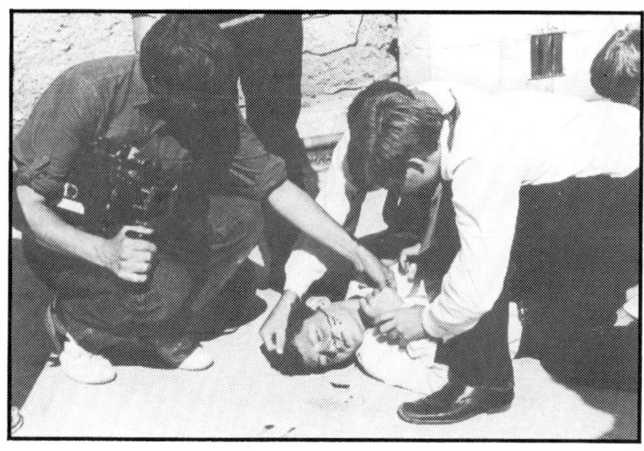

Director and cameraman Bruce Allen during the Carmi attack scene.

Russian school boys, played by boys from the Anglican school in Jerusalem. Carmi Elbert (reclining) is played by Amit Chai.

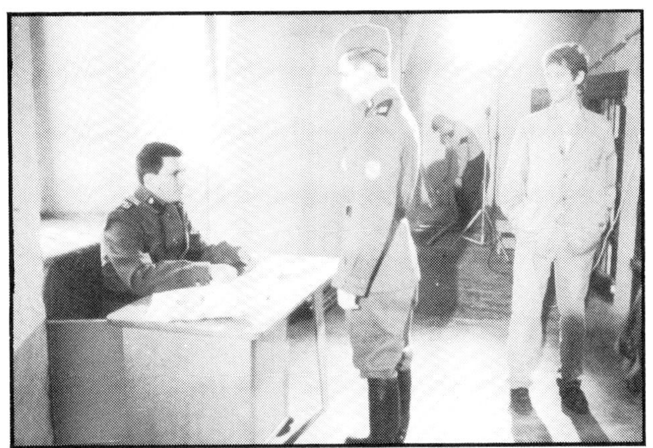

During filming of **Gates of Brass** prison sequence, in Jerusalem.

A break in filming of drug plant scene. All smiles with the KGB with director Bruce Allen (second from right) and Jay Rawlings, producer (right).

Filming during the 'forest sequence' near Jerusalem.

Jay beside director Bruce Allen (seated) and part of the crew during 'forest sequence'.

wanted a part in blessing the Jews and went about raising several thousand dollars in a rather unique way. They created a play depicting the plight of the Jews in Russia and recreated scenes of stories that Jay and I had told about our visits with them. These students and career people were among thousands who entered into the Esther Fast in April, 1983.

I am reminded of an old Norwegian friend who spent his life as a teacher in Korea. We met him very unexpectedly in Jerusalem. He was in his late 70's and was on a tour of Israel. I was concerned that he had lost weight and had a heavy cold. When I questioned where he was staying he said, "at the youth hostel in Haifa". His face lit up into a gigantic smile that melted my heart as he encouraged Jay and I in our work and then slipped something into my Bible. Later in the car I opened it and there was a 10,000 kroner bill. I burst into tears and asked Jay, "Why is it always these kind of people who give?, the ones who can least afford it". His quiet reply, " . . . because they have suffered".

Countless others gave sacrificially, such as one elderly couple from England, who forfeited their long awaited trip to Jerusalem to the Christian Celebration of the Feast of Tabernacles. Instead of making this trip of a life-time, they put their savings towards the film. Joe and Sandy Lewis, founders of "Maranatha Farms" in West Virginia have graciously hosted us on several occasions and have also donated generously to this production. Special mention must be made of the continuous prayer and financial support to Meridel and I over the years and during this film project from to Trinity

Christian Centre led by Pastor John Stone in Victoria B.C. Canada.

It is impossible to mention the hundreds of wonderful stories behind the financial response to **"Gates of Brass"**. Please forgive us if you have not been mentioned but remember the Lord keeps good records.

An orthodox Rabbi of the largest synagogue in Johannesburg said, "Jay, there are many in my congregation who want to give to this project, but I understand that you want it to be a gift to the Jewish community. However, please allow us the privilege of at least underwriting half of the premiere costs here when it comes".

Once, during a flight to London, I was seated beside a wealthy Jewish manufacturer of china. He asked how we were raising funds for the film and laughed when I said, "only by donations". "It will never work" he said, "you need investors . . . ".

Through these faithful gifts we have paid the bills monthly. Never have we had much money on hand, but just enough to pay each bill as it arose. To those of you who have participated, we want to say, **"Thank You!"** By your faithfulness you are involved in the miracle which we believe will have a direct part to play in the release of our Jewish friends from behind the Iron Curtain.

Phase 6 – Post Production

Beginning in January 1985 Bruce and Moira were heavily involved in the post-production phase. This is an enormously time-consuming and difficult period of the production. Most people think the work is done when the photography is completed. Nothing could be farther from the truth.

Our project had one other factor which

complicated matters even more. And that was that everything had been shot in Russian. The reason for this was that while in Russia we didn't want to tip off the KGB eavesdroppers; and while in Israel, we didn't want to hinder the people we interviewed since all of them were native Russian speakers. We did not want to limit their ability to express themselves because of a language barrier. This made for better content in the long run, but it made it difficult during the interviews and later to know exactly what their responses were. We were ably assisted by our Russian interviewer, Rena Levinson. All of our translation from Russian to English was done by Stefani Hoffman. Once all the interviews were translated, then both the Russian and English versions had to be numbered identically for the selection of the best segments. This alone took one week of painstaking labour.

All of the best 'takes' of the dramatic sequences had to be edited and rough assemblies made. The stock shots had to be selected and subsequent interviews shot.

Then the music score and special effects and titles all had to be arranged. Twenty-eight different pieces of music were created for the film. Special thanks to Merla Watson for the creation of 'Anatoly's Theme', from which we drew inspiration.

Next came the narration and the narrator was hired. All this along with editing time in special editing suites is very costly. Hence, during this phase, Meridel and I continued to go out on speaking tours, raising funds for the completion of the overall project.

Phase 7 – Film Release

This book and the film are being completed at exactly the same time. Twenty-seven months after the initial stages were formulated on a napkin over breakfast in a Toronto restaurant with Bruce and Moira Allen. The film's world premiere was held in the Jerusalem Theatre, Jerusalem, July 25th 1985.

Phase 8 – Distribution

The distribution of a film is as big a job as the actual production phases. This is a complex operation with many facets, but is extremely important in putting the message of the film before as many people as possible. For this reason, we have hired a specialist to do an in-depth study of the potential markets for **Gates of Brass.**

It is also the time in a formal production when the investors are rewarded for their faith in the producer, should the film be successful. In our case we had decided from the very beginning that it would be a non-profit production. However this does not mean that we should abandon good business principles and not do our best to re-invest the original funds donated. We have decided to purchase television time for a world-wide release of 'Gates of Brass' for Passover 1986. Funds will also go into the cost of dubbing the film into other languages, and to finance future films.

This latter decision is imperative, since Meridel and I have spent more than two years of our lives trying to raise the budget for **Gates of Brass** notwithstanding the long periods of separation for our family and home.

Before leaving this section I'd like to make one other point about distribution for **Gates of Brass.**

Most film subjects are rather passive and entertainment oriented. This film is different. It deals with the life and death of a people, the Soviet Jews. You can make a difference in your area. You can arrange to have the film shown in your local community centre, public library, church, synagogue, school or university, service club or fraternal organization. More details are given on how YOU can help in Chapter 8.

5

The Enemy

The Bear's Claw – The KGB

The letters "KGB" are an acronym for the Russian words *Komitet Gosudarstvenoy Bezoposnosti* which means "Committee for State Security". The KGB has a two-fold function. First it operates as a *secret* political "police" force within the Soviet Union; and secondly as a covert instrument of foreign subversion. Its sole purpose is to impose the will of the Soviet totalitarian system on people, either within or outside the USSR.

The KGB was founded on December 20th 1917, shortly after the October 25th Revolution, not by the legal basis of decree, but simply by resolution. This was done as an emergency action by Lenin himself to quell a massive uprising and a nationwide strike engineered by counter-revolutionary forces. Lenin, as the head of the All Russia Central Executive Committee appointed Felix Dzerzinsky to head the "Cheka" which was to function as a safeguard against undesirable elements intending to bring down the Bolsheviks. Actually what was birthed was an Orwellian monster that has sanctioned terror, murder, and human slavery on the unprecedented scale to ensure the survival of the 'proletariat' or the very people that it crushed. In fact the claws outgrew the "Bear" and embodied the absolute worst aspects of the saying, "the end justifies the means" no matter how terrible, sadistic and barbaric. Lenin was a believer in using terror as a political force and quickly expanded the Cheka to have powers of summary arrest, trial and execution. Furthermore it was vested with powers to incarcerate Soviet citizens in hellish concentration camps, which continually grew in number until today thousands of prisons, labour camps, and psychiatric hospitals hold approximately 5 million prisoners in the infamous Gulag Archipelego.

In the early 1920's famine was endemic in Soviet Russia, as it had been for centuries; and often in the food-growing areas 20 or 30 hostages were selected from the wealthier inhabitants. If excess food was not collected for distribution they were shot. Some 500,000 people were killed in this way, giving rise to the term "Red Terror" for the Cheka forces. Lenin's agent, Felix Dzerzhinsky, was appointed Cheka head and said in enthusiastic obedience to this master's plans, "We terrorize the enemies of the Soviet Government in order to stifle crime at its inception".[1]

Soon the excesses of the Cheka were reported to the outside world with whom Lenin wanted to establish economic relations. Thus, an outward reform was necessary. The Cheka was abolished giving rise to a series of titular changes from GPU,

[1] *Brian Freemantle,* ***KGB – The Stunning Inside Story,*** *(London: Futura Books, 1984), p. 22.*

OGPU, GUGB, NKVD, MGB; and since 1954 the KGB. Always it has been the "Sword and Shield of the Party", the shield which protects the Soviet Communist Party oligarchy and the sword by which this oligarchy[1] attempts to impose its will within and outside the Soviet Union.[2]

The series of men who headed the KGB from its inception are infamous, from Dzerzhinsky at the beginning to Beria in the Stalin Era's "Great Purge", and eventually to Andropov, from 1967 to 1982. They and others have succeeded in building "the biggest spy machine the world has ever seen".[3] The cost in human terms has been staggering. From the inception of the Cheka contemporary KGB estimates range from 10 million to 60 million Soviet citizens who have been liquidated by this terror network. Probably the real figure will never be known.

"At a New Year celebration party in 1918, Dzerzhinsky got drunk. Weeping, he wandered about in the Kremlin reception room confronting Lenin and other revolutionaries, saying again and again, 'I have spilt so much blood that I no longer have any right to live'.[4] Like Soviet historians, the KGB is selective in what it cares to remember. Dzerzhinsky's remark is not part of its folklore. For once a Soviet security man was being too honest.

In reading this you may say, "Oh, well, this could happen 50 or 60 years ago, but it surely doesn't occur today". This could not be farther from the truth. The statement "everyone suffers in the

[1] *Oligarchy means the rule of many by a few.*

[2] *John Barron,* ***KGB Today – The Hidden Hand*** *(Coronet Edition, 1984), p. 7.*

[3] *Freemantle,* ***KGB****, p. 35.*

[4] *Ibid., p. 34.*

Soviet Union",[1] is not an exaggeration. The KGB is the Soviet Union and without its omnipresent supervision of every aspect of Russian life, the totalitarian Union of Soviet Socialist Republics would cease to exist.[2]

The presence of the KGB militia is inescapable. Operating with both uniformed and plainclothes agents, its task is to guard the 41,595 miles of the Soviet frontiers and coastline. It effectively seals the borders and then it begins to concentrate on internal matters. Through its system of informers a gigantic secret network exists and defies description. Carefully placed officials watch every walk of life from schools, universities, factories, government ministries, industries, agriculture, housing developments and the permitted arts for any sign of betrayal.

The media is totally controlled by censors, including radio, television, newspapers, magazines, books and now video cassettes.

The KGB controls the police and the military. Since the time of Beria the actual administration of prison camps has been split from the KGB, but the power over these institutions remains. "In every city, town, village and hut cluster hamlet, the KGB has established informant networks to investigate the behaviour and attitude of the nation's population of more than 262 million people".[3]

How does this enormous operation really work? The lynch-pin of the entire system is the internal passport. At the age of 16 every Soviet citizen is obliged to apply for this document, for without it he

[1] *Mark Azbel,* ***Refusenik – Trapped in the Soviet Union*** *(London, New York, Toronto: MacMillan.)*

[2] *Freemantle,* ***KGB*** *p. 35.*

[3] *Barron,* ***KGB Today*** *p. 21.*

is neither allowed to work or travel about or to find housing. Here economic control is the bottom line. The section that relates to his employment or income is called the 'workbook'. In it is recorded his or her wage, job title, salary, place of employment, status, and recommendations or complaints by his or her respective employer. Also included is information as to whether a person is pure Russian or one of the 14 internal nationalities or **evri** which is Russian for Jewish.

In every work place, office, factory or collective, there are KGB officials who, as eyes and ears of the State, record the employee's progress. Anyone who for any reason is deemed undesirable is then fired. Once a person is severed from their workplace, it is next to impossible to fit into a new job, unless it is extremely degrading. Thus the person becomes a 'parasite' on the Soviet society, eligible for a prison sentence or internal exile, or hard labour at a concentration camp. In this way a large part of the Soviet labour force is found in prison.

The system works very well to police the masses by fear and intimidation. There are exceptions; but the inmates are either political prisoners, hardened criminals or those with religious convictions. They are interned in prisons, labour camps, and/or psychiatric hospitals.

The Marxist philosophy of Communism as interpreted by Lenin and inherited by the Soviet system does not allow for real freedom of religion, nor belief in the teachings of the Bible or faith in God. Some of the hardest hit under this dictatorial system are Jews and Christians who are observant and who want to teach biblical principles to their children. This is seen as an extremely dangerous poison in the Soviet social fabric and must be dealt with severely. Leaders in the Jewish and Christian communities are singled out and given harsh prison sentences to frighten others from becoming followers or expressing their beliefs. Especially hated by the KGB are the 'underground' churches and Jews with "Zionist ideals". A book has come out by the known anti-Semite mouthpiece Korneev, stating that the "enemies" of the Soviet people are Baptists, Pentecostals, and Zionists.

The enormous costs of operating the KGB internally are unknown to the West, but the CIA estimated in 1980 that the total spent on propaganda and covert action abroad was $3.4 billion.

Western intelligence experts estimate that inside the USSR there is a supervisory and administrative staff of 90,000 KGB officials and 1,500,000 agents and informers. Abroad the KGB is estimated to have 250,000 agents working undercover as embassy, consulate, delegation, airline, and trade personnel.

They also hire traitorous nationals and infiltrate 'sleepers' who are specially trained Russian nationals with false identities who live many years in a community before engaging in espionage activity.

The bear-like appetite of the Soviet system for Western military information and technology is frightening. In the last few years the Soviets have successfully stolen much of the design and engineering expertise of America's most sophisticated military apparatus. Anything goes in this world of treachery and underground activity.

Unfortunately Western diplomats and governmental bodies dealing with the Soviets have consistently underestimated the ways and means of this malignancy.

Now the most sophisticated surveillance equipment available such as microwave, satellite and laser technology is being used by the Soviets to monitor even telephone conversations of the Pentagon and high tech industry in the USA, Canada, Japan and Western Europe.

The Soviets will literally try anything to obtain Western information; to wit, the Soviet spy submarines off the coast of Scandinavia, spy trawlers along the coast of Canada, the USA and Korea, and their covert activities in Africa, Cuba and Central America. These efforts are bolstered by the KGB counterparts from the Eastern Block countries and their efforts are continuous and global in strategy. We need to pray for our leaders and ask God to give them divine wisdom in dealing with the Soviet and Eastern Block countries in their tricky negotiations.

Joseph Stalin summed up the aim of Soviet diplomacy when he said:

'Words have no relation to action, otherwise what kind of diplomacy is it? Words are one thing, actions another. Good words are a mask for concealment of bad deeds. Sincere diplomacy is no more possible than dry water or a wooden iron.'[1]

Traditionally the KGB has spent huge amounts of money on propaganda both internally and externally, more than $3 billion in 1980 alone. It is important for the Soviet ideology to be made palatable to its own citizens as well as in the international arena. One way this is attempted is

[1] *Freemantle, **KGB** p. 35.*

through the print media, especially by choosing 'scapegoat weaknesses' in the Western democracies.

Several years ago 'cosmopolitan' was the word that was chosen to illustrate the failings of the capitalists. Anyone who was cosmopolitan was given over to greed, jealousy, and selfishness. For cosmopolitans gaining wealth was the primary objective in life. This vice had to be purged from the world and the Soviets were the ones to accomplish this in messianic fashion. The problem was that the theory didn't work. The grandiose promises of the Soviet leaders of the 1960s didn't materialize by the '80s; and the hopes and the expectations of the Soviet people were only appeased by turning to their own cosmopolitan and underground capitalist system, the ubiquitous black market.

A comparison of past Soviet promises with the realities of today dramatizes the severity of current problems. At the Twenty-Second Congress in 1961, the Communist Party solemnly proclaimed that by the year 1980 the Soviet Union would achieve the utopia of "true" Communism, as the party officials promised and explained through all available media at countless assemblies, in schools, factories, farms and offices. True Communism would flood the land with a super-abundance of goods and services, all material things anyone could desire. The cornucopia of quality food, housing, clothing, appliances, automobiles, taxis and other transport, medicine and medical care, educational, cultural and recreational facilities would enable all citizens irrespective of status, occupation, age, sex, ethnic origin or locale, to partake of whatever they wanted in any quantity desired. Everything would be free.

Better still, true Communism would reform human nature and bring about the final stage in human evolution by creating the New Communist Man, the perfect being. Daily gratification of all material needs and wants would permanently purge human beings of imperfections such as greed, avarice, duplicity, jealousy, selfishness, miserliness, infidelity, and indolence. The resultant New Communist Man would be noble, altruistic, honest, courageous, strong, compassionate and comradely. Obviously and inevitably with the advent of true Communism and the New Communist Man crime, alcoholism, and all other social ills inherited from capitalism would forever vanish. Endlessly repeated in all seriousness during the 1960s, these Party promises of the millenium were heard less and less in the 1970s and not at all as 1980 approached. In light of the actual conditions prevailing in the 1980s, their repetition would constitute a kind of black comedy.[1]

Thus a new scapegoat was needed. This time it was the perennial target of Russian hatred, the Jews. Through Brezhnev's final years and Andropov's short-lived reign of fresh anti-Semitic poison, the trends hearkened back to the days of Stalin. This time the scapegoat catch-phrase was "Zionists." The ills of Soviet society could be conveniently blamed on those disloyal Jews who wanted to go to Israel, the 'Nazi-like' state in the Middle East. This concept was readily accepted by the masses and took the pressure of internal criticism off the Kremlin.

Under Andropov the KGB was reorganized. A

[1] *Barron, **KGB Today** p. 21.*

separate directorate or department was created to hound the Jews, persecute religious believers, eradicate the self-expression of underground publishing and silence dissidence. The rooting out of ideological heresy became much more systematic, scientific and effective than at any time since the death of Stalin.

Anti-Zionist propaganda filled the press, radio, and television networks. In early 1983 a group of 'puppet' Jews, the anti-Zionist Committee, was formed. The members were put on prime-time television to tell the Russian people that there were no more Jews who wanted to leave the Soviet Union and that any pockets of disloyal "Zionist Cancers" must be reported immediately to the authorities. Books were then published saying that Zionism and Nazism were the same thing and that in the 1930s and 40s Hitler had paid the Jews to go to Israel but they didn't go, so he had to liquidate them as less than human. The genesis of this mendacious concept and ultimate anti-Semitic slam linking Zionism and Nazism came from the UN when in 1975 a Resolution was passed equating Zionism to racism. The Russians had the Third World nations exactly where they wanted them by adopting anti-Zionist and anti-Israeli attitudes.

This wave of hatred against Jews was fanned intentionally by picking up on the Middle East situation, saying that the Zionist expansionists in Lebanon were backed by the US imperialists. This then justified the appalling violations by the Soviets of such international accords on human rights as the Helsinki Final Act and the UN Charter of Human Rights.

Then the real tragedy of Western silence and

indifference struck. In 1984 Dr. Andrei Sakharov, one of the world's greatest scientists and winner of the Lenin Prize, was abducted and placed in internal exile and force-fed during a hunger strike. His condition and whereabouts were unknown for weeks. His demands for emergency medical treatment abroad for his wife went unanswered by the Soviet authorities. The West was impotent to do anything on his behalf.

Here is a perfect example of Soviet ability to do absolutely whatever they like. Such treatment of victims goes unhindered when the West fails to lodge protests. The Soviets use a system called 'wait and see'. They will effect calculated violations of human rights agreements and determined maltreatment of their so-called disloyal subjects and then wait and see what the response will be internationally. If there is general apathy and no protests, then the next time they can go a step further in their game of harassment for purposes of re-education.

In a revealing article by British historian, Professor Martin Gilbert, entitled, **Appalling Record of the Andropov Era**, which appeared in the February 15 1984 **Jerusalem Post**, he points out five ways in which Soviet Jewry suffered under former KGB head Yuri Andropov.

During that time the gates of emigration were shut, crushing the morale of the emigration movement in general. Persecutions, trials and harsh sentencing of Jewish Hebrew teachers began. For instance, Yosef Begun was given thirteen years hard labour. This began to crush individuals. No former Prisoners of Zion were allowed to leave. Finally he pointed out stepped-up attacks that occured in the press against the Jewish leaders of the emigration movement and Israel itself. Since this article was published the conditions have gone from bad to worse, and today western Kremlin watchers are using the term 'neo-Stalinism' to describe the frightening trends in the Soviet Union.[1]

Two press conferences were carried out in the USSR during 1984 that hearkened back to the days of World War II Germany. The anti-Zionist Committee, headed by a traitorous Jew, General David Dragunsky, lied on national television in April 1984, saying that all disloyal Jews had left the Soviet Union and now all those who remained were happy to do so. He stated that the program of reunification of Jewish families was complete.

This falsification was easily exposed by the fact that more than 400,000 Jews in the USSR have applied to come home to Israel and have been denied. In fact these 400,000 are being arrested, harassed, intimidated and tortured today. Moreover tens of thousands have received official refusals and have become refuseniks. The Soviets now side-step the embarassing issue of protesting refuseniks by simply not granting refusals and thereby saying there are no more refuseniks.

Also blatantly untrue is the statement that all families have been reunited as nearly every one of the 400,000 Jews who would like to leave Russia have to have family in Israel who have extended an invitation for their reunification. This obliterates the idea that all families are reunited. This deception was obvious at a recent Conference of the Union of Councils of Soviet Jews held in

[1] *"Soviet Jews: Emigration is Over," **The Washington Post** 4 November 1984.*

Jerusalem where Soviet Jewish immigrants reported tearfully the horrible trauma of their separation from their loved ones for up to 12 years. This injustice has been engineered by the KGB.

Then in October 1984 a second press conference was staged on Russian television by the same Soviet Anti-Zionist Committee. This time their rhetoric was unbelievably worse. They had concocted the idea that Zionism and Nazism were one and the same and that Hitler and the Zionists had co- operated in the Holocaust in order to gain world sympathy for their cause of world dominion. Whereas anti-Semites previously denied the very existence of the Holocaust as a Jewish plot, now since the evidence of its existence is overwhelming, they twist the truth to an incredible degree to link previous enemies as one and the same. This enormous lie now gives them false ground to futher implicate the evils of the Jewish-Zionist-Israeli-American Imperialist collusion aimed at world dominion. The material on the following pages collaborates this statement in an alarming fashion.

...nti-Zionism =
...nti-Semitism
...nti-Semitism in the USSR

למען אחי ורעי

המועצה הציבורית למען יהודי ברית המועצות

THE ISRAEL PUBLIC COUNCIL FOR SOVIET JEWRY

MATERIAL PREPARED BY THE ISRAEL PUBLIC COUNCIL FOR SOVIET JEWRY., NOW MADE AVAILABLE TO THE UNION OF COUNCILS FOR SOVIET JEWS.
TRANSLATED BY THE UNION OF COUNCILS FOR SOVIET JEWS.

Dear Sir/Madame,

The Public Council For Soviet Jewry is issuing a new series of publications, the purpose of which is to bring to the attention of the Israeli public the existence of Soviet propaganda aimed at the State of Israel, the people of Israel, and the Zionist movement.

This propaganda, in its various forms, is flooding the pages of the Soviet press, which in turn is distributed to the homes of hundreds of millions of Soviet citizens. It is also transmitted on the radio and on special television programs. This propaganda serves as material at political lectures and party gatherings, where participation is compulsory for the Soviet citizen It is compiled in the form of books, "scientific research," pamphlets, and leaflets; frequently distributed (free of charge) at airports and hotels across the Soviet Union, and translated into many foreign languages.

This series of publications will assist you in recognizing the dimensions, content, and language of Soviet propaganda. We are convinced that you will then better understand the situation of Soviet Jews, forced to live day by day and hour by hour in the shadow of this propaganda campaign.

ZIONISM – A THREAT TO PEACE AND THE SECURITY OF NATIONS

a statement by the Soviet Anti-Zionist Committee.

23.11.84

The executive of the Anti-Zionist Committee of Soviet Public Opinion.

1.12.84 - "New Times" - the Source.

ZIONISM - A THREAT TO PEACE & SECURITY OF NATIONS

STATEMENT BY THE ANTI-ZIONIST COMMITTEE OF SOVIET PUBLIC OPINION, ADOPTED NOVEMBER 23, 1984

In its global offensive against peace and the security of the peoples, against the forces of social progress, the most reactionary wing of imperialism is making active use of international Zionism.

The political course steered by Israel and the subversive activity of the international Zionist centres are subordinated to the strategic interests of imperialism. By virtue of its aggressive essence and orientation, Zionism is not interested in peace and stability, in building trust among peoples.

On behalf of the broad masses of the Soviet public, united in whose ranks are all the nations and nationalities of the U.S.S.R., which constitute a new historical community, the Soviet people, our Committee declares:

ZIONISM TODAY IS BELLICOSE CHAUVINISM AND RACIAL INTOLERANCE

Which find concentrated expression in the genocide practised by the Israeli ruling upper stratum against the Palestinian Arab people in Israel, the occupied Arab territories and Lebanon. The massacre staged by the henchmen of the Israeli aggressors in September 1982 in the Palestinian refugee camps of Sabra and Shatila in Western Beirut was possible only with the direct complicity of the Israeli army.

ZIONISM TODAY IS A CULT OF PERMISSIVENESS AND IMPUNITY IN POLITICS.

For the rulers of Israel it has long been standard practice to ignore the generally recognized principles of international law. The systematic and openly provocative disregard of the will of the international community as expressed in numerous United Nations decisions is arousing the anger of people. The Zionists persistently continue to deny the Arab people of Palestine their inalienable right to self-determination and to their own statehood-a right proclaimed by the U.N. General Assembly on November 29, 1947.

ZIONISM TODAY MEANS THOUSANDS UPON THOUSANDS OF WRECKED HUMAN LIVES IN ISRAEL ITSELF

Morally corrupting primarily the young people, the Israeli rulers send them to slaughter innocent women, children and old people. Many of those who have fallen into the Zionist trap have met their end in the ranks of the Israeli army.

The danger of fascism is steadily growing in Israel. As the Israeli parliamentary election of July 1984 showed, Zionism is moving more and more to the Right-towards increasing intensive use of open Nazi, racist methods in both the foreign and the domestic policy of the State of Israel. Deputies from the ultra-Right nationalist party Tehiya sit in the Knesset, the Israeli parliament. Even the terrorist rabbi, Meir Kahane, who preaches bellicose racism, is a Knesset deputy.

ZIONISM TODAY IS CONSISTENT SUPPORT OF THE MOST DIEHARD QUARTERS OF THE INTERNATIONAL IMPERIALIST REACTION.

Israel, acting as a tool of imperialism in the Middle East, seeks to crush the Arab national liberation movement. Among Tel Aviv's friends and allies are the fascist military dictatorship in Chile, the stranglers of the people in El Salvador, the Nicaraguan contras, the South African racists, and other anti-democratic regimes which it lavishly supplies with up-to-date weapons.

ZIONISM TODAY IS ANTI-DETENTE

The Israeli and international Zionist centres, cynically posing as exponents of the interests of the Jews of different countries of the world, have actively joined in a "crusade" against socialism and are obstructing all efforts to improve the international climate. Assuming the role of self-appointed "defenders" of the Soviet Jews and resorting to lies, slander and fabrications, they are trying to interfere in the internal affairs of the Soviet Union, to raise artificial barriers to mutual understanding among nations.

ZIONISM TODAY IS UNDISGUISED EMPHASIS ON INDIVIDUAL AND STATE TERRORISM.

Tel Aviv has mounted a foul terrorist campaign against representatives of the Palestine Liberation Organization in third countries.

People who are unwilling to submit to Zionist diktat are constantly terrorized morally by international Zionist organizations, under cover of which the Israeli special services operate.

Israel uses against the Palestinian and other Arab peoples typically Gestapo killing methods, torture, concentration camps.

ZIONISM TODAY IS UNCEASING WAR.

In the less than 40 years of the existence of Israel, neighbouring Arab countries have five times been subjected to Israeli aggression. As a result, the Middle East has been made a seat of chronic military tension. Ever since the establishment of the Israeli state in 1948, Tel Aviv has been pursuing a policy of territorial expansion and justification of annexation. The refusal of the Israeli government to withdraw from the occupied Arab territories, including East (Arab) Jerusalem, is one of the main obstacles to the establishment of just and lasting peace in the region.

The weaponry used by the Israeli army includes cluster and vacuum bombs, chemical weapons, booby traps for use against non-combatants - including booby traps in the shape of toys, a barbarous means of killing children - in other words, means of warfare which are strictly banned by international law.

ZIONISM TOMORROW IS THE THREAT OF NUCLEAR CONFLICT IN THE MIDDLE EAST.

Israel refuses to accede to the treaty on the non-proliferation of nuclear weapons. The Israeli government hypocritically declares that Israel will not be the first Middle East country to use these weapons. Yet there is every reason to assume that Tel Aviv already now possesses nuclear weapons and in the future will make use of the threat to employ mass destruction weapons; that is, will pursue a policy of nuclear blackmail and terror. The irresponsible policy of Israel, which is giving effect to the strategic plans of Washington, is turning the Middle East into "the Balkans of a third world war."

WE ADDRESS THIS APPEAL TO ALL HONEST-MINDED MEN AND WOMEN ON OUR PLANET, TO ALL WHO CHERISH WORLD PEACE:
JOIN THE STRUGGLE AGAINST INTERNATIONAL ZIONISM, TAKE ACTION AGAINST THE AGGRESSIVE EXPANSIONIST POLICY OF ISRAEL IN THE MIDDLE EAST!
FOR THE SAKE OF PEACE ON EARTH! FOR THE SAKE OF THE SECURITY OF NATIONS!

The Anti-Zionist Committee of Soviet Public Opinion was founded on April, 1, 1984 by a "group of Sovie citizens". The head of the committee is the Soviet army general David Dragunsky and members of th committee are writers, journalists and academicians. The members of the executive committee are engage in wide public activities, article publications, mass-media interviews. The main purpose of the abov activities is condemnation of the Zionist ideology, comparison of Nazi ideology to Israeli policy in all spheres especially in the sphere of the solution of the Israeli-Arab conflict.

The main activity of this committee, its essence and reason for foundation is to deny the right of the State c Israel to fight for Soviet Jews, and to deny any attachment between Jews in the USSR and the State of Israe

ISRAELI INVADERS IN LEBANON

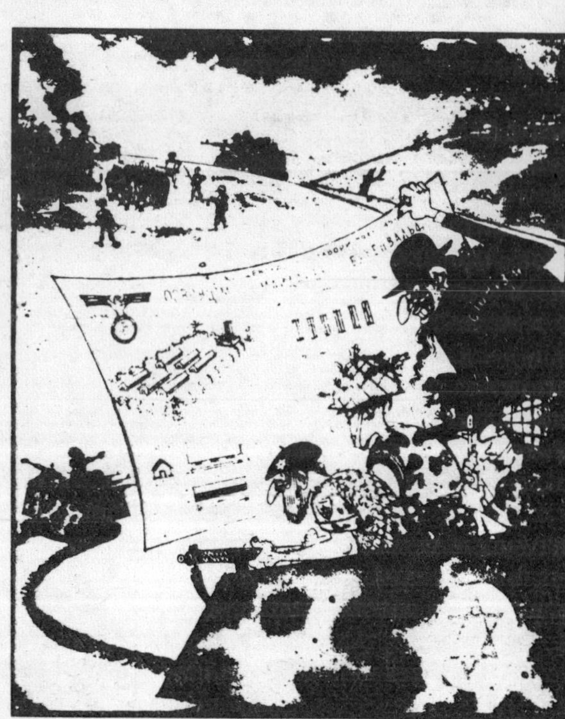

Start to build concentration camps, according to these plans, they have already proven themselves once
On the back of the Jew is written "Zionism".
On the map: Concentration camps Aushwitz, Maidanek, Buchenwald.

June, 1983

ithout comment . . .
Anti-Semitism in the USSR

למען אחי ורעי
המועצה הציבורית למען יהודי ברית המועצות
THE ISRAEL PUBLIC COUNCIL FOR SOVIET JEWRY

MATERIAL PREPARED BY THE ISRAEL PUBLIC COUNCIL FOR SOVIET JEWRY., NOW MADE AVAILABLE TO THE UNION OF COUNCILS FOR SOVIET JEWS. TRANSLATED BY THE UNION OF COUNCILS FOR SOVIET JEWS.

THE CHIEF OF THE THIEVES SHOWS HIS GUILT

Directorate of the Soviet Anti Zionist Committee

These are their words;

"There are solid facts that tesify to the collaboration between the Zionists and the Nazis." "Even today, the Israeli agrressors are using methods, typical of the Nazis, such as the advocation of racism, which is a part of the Zionist ideology and becomes the normal policy of Israeli state terror." From a press conference held by the Soviet anti-Zionist Committee: "The Criminal Alliance between the Zionists and the Nazis," 12.10.84

AND THESE ARE THEIR DEEDS:

FIND THE DIFFERENCE

NAZI PROPAGANDA SOVIET PROPAGANDA

NAZI PROPAGANDA SOVIET PROPAGAND

CAUSES
DIVISION
AMONG
NATIONS

NAZI PROPAGANDA

SOVIET PROPAGANDA

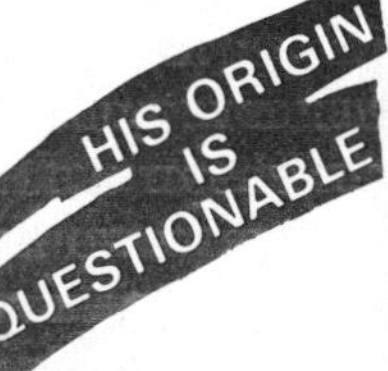

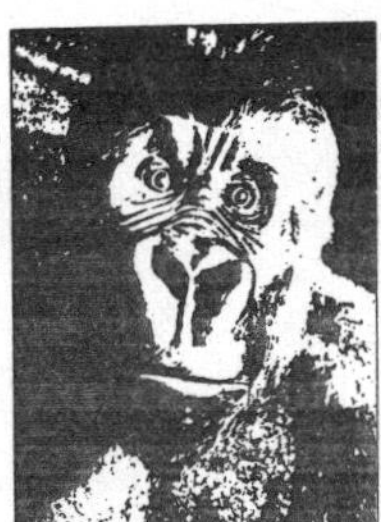

RULES THE WORLD THROUGH A WORLD-WIDE JEWISH-ZIONIST-MASONIC CONSPIRACY

Н. В. ПОКОРМЯК

АРМИЯ ИЗРАИЛЯ—
ОРУДИЕ
ИМПЕРИАЛИСТИЧЕСКОЙ
АГРЕССИИ

Ордена Трудового Красного Знамени
ВОЕННОЕ ИЗДАТЕЛЬСТВО
МИНИСТЕРСТВА ОБОРОНЫ СССР
МОСКВА · 1977

Nikolai Vassilevich Pokormiak

ISRAEL'S ARMY-THE TOOL OF IMPERIALIST AGGRESSION

Moscow,
The Defense Ministry Publication, Moscow

"There is no end to the list of beastly acts committed by the Israeli militarists against the Arabs. When the acts of aggression; in June 1967, the Israeli soldiers were given an order: "Do not take prisoners." Later, when the international community heard of the existence of this atrocious order, the Tel Aviv Command tried to characterize it as a "humanitarian act." But Israeli soldiers accepted this order as an incentive for their acts of brutality and mass murder, even boasting in their conversations of the number of slain Arab captives ...

"In the Syrian village of Manshura, Israeli soldiers gathered all the inhabitants left alive in a house, poured gasoline on it, and burnt everyone ...

"The crimes of the Israeli robbers on Lebanese soil are well known. In the village of Rafid, a mother and her seven children, aged one to fifteen, were killed, their bodies lying underneath the ruins of their house. In the village of Juhea, an Israeli officer ordered a passenger car, still containing the passengers, to be steamrolled over. Amongst them were two children, in jured earlier by an Israeli bombardment. Blood-covered bodies and a few sheets of tin, were the only remnants of the car and its passengers ...

"... A captured Israeli pilot testified: "We were ordered to bomb civilian targets. The order I received was: "Bomb Damascus, every target, every location." These atrocities of Israeli military personnel go unpunished. The soldier is consciously 'relieved' of all doubts concerning the justice of murdering peaceful civilians."

"The Israeli aggressors 'have put out of mind' the Geneva Convention; they have forgotten the Nuremberg trials that were held not so long ago; they should have remembered that in Tel Aviv ...

"The Israeli soldiers, who are insolent against defenseless civilians, panic and show their cowardice in more difficult and complicated situations. Such was the case in October 1973 when during a period of massive assaults by the Israeli Air Force against Syria and Egypt, there were frequent hits by Arab anti-aircraft missiles. A group of Israeli pilots, fearing for their lives, refused to go out on a combat mission. The High Command took an unprecedented measure, unheard of in Israel-eight pilots who revealed their cowardice were executed by a firing squad before their comrades ...

"Intensive and daily ideological brainwashing, performed by experienced professionals using the mass media and other modern technological methods, allow the Israeli military to imbue the soldiers with a spirit of blind obedience to orders, hatred towards any progress, and cruely and aggression towards the Arab people. Being poisoned by chauvinist racist slogans, the soldiers and officers of the Israeli Army are not only victims of Zionism, but act as the Storm Troopers of this movement. To secure Zionist goals, they will not hesitate to commit any crime, any evil against the Arab nations. These acts are no less cruel than the atrocities committed by the Fascist conquerors in World War II, or those of the American soldiers in Indo-China. The moral character of the Israeli conquerors is no better than that of the S.S. personnel or the American Sadists of My Lai in Vietnam."

NAZI PROPAGANDA

SOVIET PROPAGANDA

The Bear's Weakness

Like any bear the Soviet Union has an acute sense of smell but it is nearly blind. This characteristic is illustrated in a variety of ways politically, socially and economically. In this section we will examine some of these shortcomings in order to correctly demonstrate ways of combating this sinister system.

Atheism

'The fool hath said in his heart, There is no God'

Psalm 14:1

The Soviet system is doomed to fail because of its own self-defeating belief that there is no God. This has been the folly of all the nations that have come against the Jewish people. The record is formidable. From Amalek throughout history to the present day, the world's most powerful human governents and military machines have ultimately collapsed on their faces, utterly destroyed in front of the God of Israel.

The God of the Communist System

The central doctine of the Marxist theory is that the will of the individual must be given up for the benefit of the State. The individual must relinquish all personal and private aspirations so that the collective good may be achieved. Then in turn all the needs of the individual will be met by the State. One the surface this appears to be a good idea, but in practice it doesn't work. Why? Because it operates completely contrary to the principles of

God. For example, God has given to every human being the divine right and gift that he will never violate the will of man. Man's ability to choose is sovereign. God gives man the freedom to either believe or not to believe in His existence.

The ultimate humanist response in this "free will" plan is to say, "I am God," replacing the Creator of the entire universe with oneself. It is interesting to remember that when Moses asked who the Lord was, he received this simple and profound answer, "**I Am**."

Thus a doctrine that denies the very fountain or source of its existence is destined to fail. The Communist system must then police itself to ensure that all its people are adhering to the concept that the State is first and foremost. They believe that anything less than 100 per cent blind obedience to this system will eventually cause the whole structure to corrupt, corrode, and eventually fall.

Enter the KGB. The KGB, the enormous system of informers, is the eyes and ears of the State. Its job is to control the population and to monitor the political attitudes and behaviour of Soviet citizens and to detect any anti-Soviet actions or statements. This is done to guarantee the loyalty of the people to the system. Thus all human freedoms held sacred and dear to the free world are sacrificed forever. Then the conflict begins, both internally and externally. First it is impossible to encapsulate the human will, proven by various sectors of the Soviet society who will not succumb. Secondly they in turn become the "enemies of the people" who must be crushed.

Enter the Gulag Archipelago. Then the injustice

of the world's largest prison system now determines the future of those Russians who dare to exercise the luxury of free will. From psycho-prisons, concentration and labour camps a few voices are able to convey to the free world this gigantic cult that employs satanic methods to preserve itself.

Enter the propaganda machine. Now the false system must tell lies about itself and others in order to maintain itself. Soon some of its own citizens begin to recognize the farce and are put in the difficult position of having to either succomb and become a mindless robot or to bravely maintain their own will and self-esteem, the latter position carrying with it the permanent threat of annihilation as traitors.

Enter the Jews and Christians. Real believers in both faiths must withstand enormous pressures to hold on to their beliefs and traditions that honour the Lord. The irony of the situation is that persecution has always made Jews and Christians stronger believers. This is true in the Soviet Union.

Enter the Bible. Here is the eternal document that disproves the Marxist ideals. The covenants of God with man as expressed by the Scriptures give humanity faith and hope. The Communists detest this power of the Holy Bible and are bent on its demise and eventual destruction.

'The grass withereth, the flower fadeth; but the word of our God shall stand forever.'

Isaiah 40:8

'Heaven and earth shall pass away, but my words shall not pass away.'

Matthew 24:35

The Enormous Facade

The above twisting of the truth to serve the objectives of the party has also extended into the international press and world politics. To protect their position the Soviets and Eastern Block countries spend billions of dollars on propaganda and go to great lengths to prove their superiority. The Soviet space program is one example of this. Here they spend billions on emulating the US achievements in outer space and yet they cannot put food into the inner space of their citizens. Also the enormous energy and effort that goes into the Soviet Olympic team is expended to prove their political superiority.

In his book **Refusenik**, Mark Azbel, a renowned physicist and former refusenik observes that:

'The majority of the populace is kept in such straightened conditions that it is hardly a figure of speech to say it is being systematically starved into submission to the will of its leaders. All the strength of the nation and of the people is concentrated on military research, on outerspace exploration, and so forth: what energy is left over goes into sports or ballet and other artistic pyrotechnics. All of the Soviet wealth is poured into areas of threat or spectacle. Under these circumstances the leadership assumes that persecutions are needed to keep all the people silent and obedient.'[1]

Having established that their system is superior and above reproach, the Soviet hierarchy thus demands total obedience from its servants. To question the leadership is considered traitorous and no-one is permitted to examine the dogmas

[1] *Azbel, **Trapped** p. 211.*

laid down by the party official. In theory the 10 per cent or so of the population that belong to the Communist party govern the masses. But in fact the USSR is ruled with an iron hand by a small group of Politburo elite. Their authority is **unquestioned** and final.

Arkady Shevchenko, the highest ranking Soviet diplomat to defect to the West since World War II, has this to say about this "fossilized elite":

'My personal reward for being Gromyko's adviser was that I became a member of the 'nomenklatura' hierarchy. This is a list of the most important posts in the party, government administration and other institutions. These positions are filled by direct party appointment or with party approval. Nomenklatura is a caste system that applies only to the elite class. Its many levels enjoy varying degrees of privilege according to rank.

For Politburo members there is no limit or restriction on privileges. Below this level the grading structure begins. The Central Committee defines the place of anyone eligible for inclusion in the various categories: high party apparatchiki, Cabinet ministers, diplomats or individuals with unusual abilities or exceptional talents such as artists, scientists, Olympic champions and the like. Factory workers, farmers, engineers, lawyers, doctors, store managers and other private citizens are excluded.

Members of the elite have extensive privileges: high salaries, good apartments, dachas, cars with chauffeurs, special railway cars and accommodation, VIP treatment at airports, resorts and hospitals off limits to outsiders, special schools for their children, access to stores selling consumer goods and food at reduced prices. They live far removed from the common man and, indeed, have to go out of their way if they wish to rub elbows with the less exalted. The highest group in the nomenklatura is separated from most citizens by a barrier as psychologically imposing as the Great Wall of China. This class constitutes virtually a state within a state.

Those designated under the system number many thousands. They form the backbone of the status quo in the governmental and social structure. They will permit no-one to transform the society or alter its foreign or domestic policy in any way that may affect their perquisites. It is no small irony to know that this fossilized elite controls the nation that calls on other countries to renounce stability for revolution, to give up privilege for the blessings of proletarianism.'[1]

The Claw in the Brain

The term "brain-washing" has been used for decades to describe tactics implemented in altering the attitudes and even thought processes of people caught up in totalitarian states. In these systems there is no room for individual privileges such as freedom of thought, speech, or belief in God. In fact, persistent violations of Soviet dogma by such thinking is deemed "presumptuous and dangerous" to the overall social stability and justify the ultimate violation of a human being, the introduction of chemicals into the mind. The cover used for this crushing of Prisoners of Conscience is the Soviet psychiatric hospitals.

In February 1984 Amnesty International

[1] *Arkady Shevchenko, "Breaking With Moscow,"* ***Time*** *February 1985, p. 26.*

published "Political Abuse of Psychiatry in the USSR," detailing the cases of 110 people who had been confined to Soviet psychiatric institutions the previous five years for peacefully exercising their human rights.

The paper analysed committing procedures resulting in the wrongful confinement of dissidents and reported specific allegations of ill-treatment given by the Soviets including beatings by hospital staff and the administration to patients of painful and disorienting drugs in excessive quantities and without necessary correctives. The paper also described the pressure applied to Prisoners of Conscience to renounce their beliefs and the punishment they received if they refused to do so.[1] The following are two recent examples of such treatment:

On December 18th 1984 Nadechka Fradkova, a Leningrad refusenik mathematician, was sentenced to two years in a labour camp for 'parasitism'. Fradkova's lawyer was prevented by the court from proving that during the time which she was accused of parasitic behaviour, she was actually being forcibly detained in a state psychiatric hospital and treated with drugs.[2]

The following very moving letter describes this horror first-hand. It was written from a Soviet mental institution by a young Russian college instructor, V.I.Chermyshov, and smuggled out. It reads:

' . . . Having been buried, it's hard to prove that you are alive, except, perhaps, if a miracle should happen and someone dug up your grave before you

[1] ***Amnesty International Report*** *(1984), p. 312.*

[2] ***Update*** *(Jerusalem, Israel: Soviet Jewry Education and Information Center, (January, February, 1985)).*

died for good. It is hard to prove one's soundness of mind from within the walls of a psychiatric hospital.

I finished the mechanical engineering-mathematics course at LSU (Leningrad State University), then worked as an instructor of maths with the title of Assistant in the Leningrad branch of the Moscow Institute. I got carried away with collecting books and records, wrote poems for myself, short stories and philosophical essays. I typed up all my writings and bound them in three note books: poems and aphorisms, short stories and abstract disserations, philosophical essays and statements of my ideas of an anti-communist nature. During my five years of writing philosophical studies, I gave them to only two people. In March 1970 I was arrested for anti-Soviet propaganda. One of the readers of my writings repented at once and was given his freedom. The other, a graduate of the Art Acadamy, V. Popov, whose guilt was in having drawn a diagram in my notebook, was arrested.

In prison I was examined for thirty minutes and a diagnosis was reached: chronic schizophrenia of a paranoid type. I didn't see a lawyer, was not present at the trial, and wasn't even told of the diagnosis or about the trial for a month and a half. My wife told me about it during a visit after the trial. The same diagnosis was given for Popov . . .

In America Angela Davis was arrested. The whole world up to now knows about her fate; she has lawyers; people protest in her favour. But **I, I have no rights** ; not once did I meet a lawyer; I wasn't present at the trial; I have no right to complain; I have no right to go on a hunger strike. I myself have seen how, in psychiatric hospitals, they tie protesting political prisoners who refuse to take food or 'medicine', give them a shot after which they cannot move and forcibly feed and 'treat' them. A man called V. Borisov has protested for the past two years. They treat him with aminazin, which results in a loss of individuality, his intellect gets blunt, his emotions are destroyed and his memory disappears. This is the death of creativity: those given aminazin cannot even read afterwards.

Even though I am afraid of death, let them rather shoot me. How vile, how repulsive is the thought that they will defile, and crush my soul!!! I appeal to believers. **Help.** N.I.Broslavsky, a Christian, has languished here for over 25 years. And Timonin, whose guilt consists solely of having poured ink in a voting urn. They jeer at Timonin's religious feelings, they demand that he repudiate his faith, otherwise they won't let him out. Stand up for their souls, Christians!!

I am afraid of death but I'll accept it. I'm terribly afraid of torture. But there is a worse torture, and it awaits me – the introduction of chemicals into my mind. The vivisectors of the 20th Century will not hesitate to seize my soul; maybe I will remain alive, but after this I won't be able to think. I have already been informed of the decision for my treatment!

Farewell?'

Andropov himself confirmed that the use of such tactics was sanctioned by the KGB when he said in a 1977 tribute to Stalin as the first chieftain of the Russian secret police, "We try to help those who are confused and try to get them to change their minds and dispel their confusion."[1]

Mass Intimidation

In order to prevent rebellious talk and even thinking, the KGB also established a mind-boggling array of 'informants' placed everywhere throughout the Soviet Union. Each echelon of the security service has its own roster of informants from the top offices in Moscow down to the town or village level. This network of unpaid KGB informants provides the party with the cheapest and most effective instrument for controlling the Soviet citizen. Good informants are often rewarded for their work.

'The KGB meets with few turndowns in recruiting informants. Party members will co-operate without hesitation. For a non-party member to refuse to assist the state in ferreting out disloyal citizens is evidence of his own disloyalty. For persons with a strong distaste for informing on their fellow workers or students, there are pressures brought to bear: a demotion, losing a job or a scholarship, getting a permanent black mark in a police dossier. Once he agrees to co-operate, however reluctantly, the informant has to play ball for his own protection. He can promise himself not to report on his friends or colleagues but he faces two problems. He is under pressure by his handler to come up with 'useful' information. When his failure to report is itself a cause for suspicion, he is bound to find something to report. And when he does hear someone say something he knows he should report, he is faced with a serious dilemma. He knows he will be tested. Did Citizen X criticize

[1] *Barron, **KGB Today** p. 21.*

the Party, or even the Leader, out of a spontaneous impulse or was he following the instruction of the KGB handler? This climate of provocation robs any man of his self- assurance'.[1]

It is in the midst of such tyranny that the real heroes of modern history are born; men who will not succumb to this game ultimately become "Prisoners of Conscience". The party hates them with a passion and must eliminate them for its own self-preservation.

How many informants the KGB had in the 40s or early 50s cannot be estimated but their number must have been formidable considering the challenges faced by the Party in restoring the controls broken up during the war, especially in the western regions. At one period in the 30s it was reasonably estimated the KGB had more than 5 million informants, a network of eyes and ears that blanketed the Soviet Union from the Ukraine to the Pacific.

A control system becomes even more effective when it enjoys the co-operation of all its citizens in monitoring each other. In the post-war atmosphere Stalin transmitted his own fears and suspicions to the entire population. The campaign against "enemies of the State" was promoted by Party propagandists and by the Soviet Press and radio. A high degree of vigilance became a patriotic duty.

The cardinal virtue of an informant system is not its size or extent but the belief of the citizenry in its existence. Once a citizen is convinced that he is surrounded by informants, it does not matter whether or not he is. If any wall has ears, perhaps it

[1] *Harry Rositzke, **The KGB – The Eyes of Russia** (London: Sedgwick & Jackson, 1982), pp. 106-107.*

is this one. An occasional notice in the press of a local denunciation or the rumour of an informant's success in the citizen's factory or apartment house will keep him on his toes.

'The effect on the ordinary man is to heighten his own sense of vulnerability. If he denounces someone else he proves his 'revolutionary' vigilanace to the authorities. His may be an honest denunciation, but meaner motives also operate: to get back at the nasty boss, a disagreeable neighbour, a rival suitor. And then there are in every society the simply evil or sadistic types, the writers of poisonous pen letters, the slightly insane who flourish in an atmosphere equating the lie with the patriot.

It is in times of such stress that the control system attains its ultimate goal: the shattered citizen. Robbed of trust in others the individual becomes isolated from his neighbours, his friends, even his family. The only route left is to make allegiance to the Party, the Army, the Trade Union.'[1]

A "1984" generation is born that unquestioningly bows down and does obeisance to the system.

Preparation For The Final False Messiah

The success of the 'social lobotomy' is evident everywhere in the Soviet Union and its satellites. The frightening fact arises that this is the groundwork for a worldwide system of control that the Bible forecasts will arise before the reign of Messiah on earth. Just before the advent of this age of peace and justice, longed for by Jews and Christians alike, is the global rule of a false messiah. This person will offer the world a

[1] *Ibid.*

counterfeit peace and social order including a one-world government and a global monetary system that will purport to solve all of mankind's financial problems. No more famine, war, or economic stress will be the promise of the ultimate control system. Like the Russian KGB, this antichrist or false messiah will control by economics. He will simply say that everyone who wants to buy and sell any item must receive a mark or number on his body. At the outset it seems simple and harmless, but it is actually a matter of life and death. Food and basic commodities will be controlled absolutely. The people who refuse to follow this leader and his system will be unable to get food and eventually starve to death. Recent developments in the world economy point to the evolution of this system. A 'one-world' cashless monetary economic scheme would suggest a solution to the incredibly complex international problems of inflation, unemployment, balance of payments, spiralling national debts, poverty, famine, and equlization of wealth. The rapid spread worldwide of credit cards, bar-code pricing, and electronic fund transfers pave the way for the false messiah's system and his reign of absolute power through the global economy. The Scriptures are clear in reference to this:

'And he causeth all, both small and great, rich and poor, free and bond, to receive a mark in their right hand or in their foreheads:

And that no man might buy or sell, save he that had the mark, or name of the beast, (antichrist) or the number of his name.

Here is wisdom. Let him that hath understanding count the number of the beast:

for it is the number of a man; and his number is six hundred three score and sixty-six.'

Revelation 13:16-18

The significance of this triple six mark or numbering system is mentioned in Dr. Mary Stuart Relfe's book entitled, **When Your Money Fails the 666 System is Here**[1] and **New Money System**[2]. These volumes outline the frightening developments worldwide preparing for the false messiah. They are compulsory reading to see how the free world economy and the communist world control tactics are going to unite to form the most powerful and ominous system of control the world has ever seen. This will be the birth of the false messiah system after a long gestation period throughout history.

In reading this some individuals may begin to fear and even panic. This is not necessary. However, we must recognise that the Bible is relevant to the world today and that its teachings and warnings must be observed. According to the prophets of God, **never** take a mark or a number on your hand or forehead. To do so is to join with the false messiah system and death.

Read the following Scriptures:

Matthew 24:21-31	Joel 3
Isaiah 63	Revelation 19:11, 20:2
Daniel 12:1	Jeremiah 30:6-9

It is interesting to note from reading these Scriptures that the Jewish nation will be the one who breaks this false system. The Jews worldwide and Israel will be duped by the burning claims of

[1] *Mary Stuart Relfe, **The New Money System** (Montgomery: Ministries Inc., 1982), p. 3.*

[2] *Ibid.*

this world leader and so will the entire earth. However, he makes one fatal mistake. When he sets himself up to be worshipped the eyes of the Jewish nation are opened and their rebellion against this blasphemy will usher onto the earth the most horrendous period of destruction in the history of mankind, called 'Jacob's Trouble,' and it will only cease when the true messiah personally destroys the counterfeit messiah and his assembled armies at Armageddon.

6

The Divine Strategy

One may ask, how does this modern exodus of Jews from Russian captivity relate to me? Where does it fit? The following material, including Chapter 7, is presented to put into focus some of the overlying principles of Divine Strategy in this regard.

Abraham becomes a Jew

'Now the Lord had said unto Abram, get thee out of thy country, and from thy kindred, and from thy father's house, unto a land that I will shew thee:

And I will make of thee a great nation, and I will bless thee, and make thy name great; and thou shalt be a blessing:

And I will bless them that bless thee, and curse him that curseth thee: and in thee shall all families of the earth be blessed.

SO ABRAM DEPARTED AS THE LORD HAD SPOKEN UNTO HIM;'

Genesis 12:1-4a

One of the most powerful illustrations of Man's obedience to God is revealed by this scripture.

Faithful Abram, in hearkening to the voice of God, began a thread of blessing that has flowed down through history until the present day. In Genesis 12:1-3 God spoke to him the seven terms of a contract or covenant and their activation was dependent on one thing . . . Abram's absolute obedience. By obeying God, Abram became the father of the Jewish nation. The very word "evri" or "Hebrew" which comes from the Hebrew root letters עבר means to "cross over". Abram and his family were called to leave the comfort and security of Chaldean society and of idol worship, to travel by faith to "a land that I will shew thee". Trusting in God, he had to "cross over" one of the earth's most treacherous and dangerous deserts through parts of Iran, Iraq, Turkey and Syria to find the land of promise. This principle of obedience in "crossing over" joined the first Hebrew to the land of promise and has not changed throughout history. Some people have helped toward the fulfilment of this contract between God and the Jew and have been blessed, while others have opposed it, therefore forfeiting the blessings of God. God has involved Himself in human history through the Abrahamic Covenant. Someone has said that prophecy is the mould into which history has been poured. Since time immemorial every generation has had the opportunity to either help or hinder the sovereign Jewish connection to their promised land.

In this section, we will briefly examine the historic forces for and against the Jews in their connection to Israel and the completion of the eternal Covenant of God with Abraham. As we closely examine what has transpired in the history of Israel and the Jewish People, we catch a glimpse of the hand of God extended into the affairs of Man. He has chosen to reveal His eternal truths to those who will look and listen to the Holy scriptures and the ever-relevant history of the Jewish nation. One can see, for example, the covenant-making and keeping character of God revealed through Abraham, the divine laws of God given through Moses, the eternal principles of a holy God for his nation executed through the prophets and people of Israel. God's plan for eternal redemption is the theme song of the Bible as exemplified in Moses, David, Jeremiah, Ezekiel, Daniel and Jesus. Through these vessels God has painted a mosaic of interdependent truth, His will and plan revealed to mankind. The sufferings and convolutions of the people of Israel recorded by history spells out principles of deliverance and redemption for all humanity.

In Jewish history, the recurring cycles of disobedience, bondage and near destruction, followed by obedience with its ensuing deliverance gives us **hope** in our generation in the face of potential nuclear annihilation, economic chaos, terror, war and human suffering. God ***is*** involved with the affairs of men.

The Great Escape

Throughout the millenia, the Jews have suffered more than any other nation, yet out of the cauldron of their pain has come the distillate of hope, despite difficulty and hardship. Four generations after Abraham received the covenant which bound the Jewish people to the land of Israel his great grandson Joseph was sold into Egyptian slavery by his hateful brothers. One act of disobedience and wilful jealousy opened the door to ten generations of bondage, this time involving the entire nation of Israel. Now in Egypt the time had come and the stage was set for a national "cross over". Through the miracle of the Red Sea believing Israelites were given the opportunity to prove themselves as those who would "cross over" on dry ground from Egypt to Canaan. Never before or since has a miracle of this magnitude occurred to prove the eternal Covenant of Abraham. When God's time for their deliverance had come, Pharaoh couldn't get rid of the Hebrews fast enough. Today, through present world events, we are seeing the ground-work being laid for an even greater miracle of Jewish release from bondage, the "crossing over" of millions of Jews from Russia to Israel.

Ten Tough Phrases

This seemingly impossible situation for the entire nation when it was thrust into the desert became the springboard for God's next revelation, the Torah or Mosaic Law. In ten phrases the Divine expectations of the love of God and love of one's fellow man became the guiding principles of the Jewish People on their way "across" the Northern Sinai towards Caanan. Then, due to the sin of murmuring against Moses and God, the entire nation "in transit" was prevented from entering the promised land, with the exception of faithful Joshua and Caleb. This national disobedience, along with Moses' and Aaron's personal disobedience, was sufficient to bring God's judgement upon that generation. Only the new believing generation qualified by their faith and obedience for entrance into Caanan. Once in the land, the Mosaic Covenant took pre-eminence.

Back to Babylon

Unfortunately the Bible reveals that disobedience and idolatry continually recurred and appeared in the very fabric of Jewish society, until finally the ten northern tribes went into dispersion and the majority of the two southern tribes of Benjamin and Judah were taken into Babylonian captivity. Disobedience separated the Jews from their land because they did not allow the land to rest one year out of every seven, according to God's commandment.This captivity returned them as a nation to the very place where God originated the call to Abraham. The captivity lasted for seventy years, at the end of which the Lord caused a Gentile ruler by the name of Cyrus to release the Jews back to their land of promise. They once again "crossed over" and came home to Zion. But this was only a remnant and the remainder were later saved from total destruction when God worked once more in history and brought deliverance to the Jewish people through Queen Esther, a Jewess. Her fasting and prayer, coupled with her uncle Mordecai's righteousness brought the evil scheme of Jewish genocide under Haman to nothing.

Judah's Second Home-Coming

The magnitude of this "cross over" miracle must be understood to be appreciated. The Lord used His prophet Isaiah, as recorded in Isaiah 45:1 and 2 to speak to Cyrus, the unbelieving Gentile ruler, the following:

'Thus saith the Lord to His anointed, to Cyrus, whose right hand I have holden, to subdue nations before him; and I will loose the loins of kings, to open before him the two leaved gates; and the gates shall not be shut;

I will go before thee, and make the crooked place straight: I will break in pieces the *gates of brass* and cut in sunder the bars of iron:

And I will give thee the treasures of darkness, and hidden riches of secret places, that thou mayest know that I, the Lord, which call thee by thy name, am the God of Israel.'

Isaiah 45:1,2,3

One must not fail to see the spiritual warfare that preceded and followed their release as a people from Babylon. Chapter nine of Daniel gives explicit details of how Daniel studied the Book of Jeremiah and understood the timings of God. He perceived that Jerusalem's seventy years of desolation were over and that Zion must be reunited with her people. Daniel had a clear understanding of the righteous ways of God and in sackcloth and ashes he cried out in repentance for the sins of himself and his people.

Thus, when God released the children of Israel from Babylon, a remnant "crossed over" once again back to the promised land. This time they were led by Ezra and Nehemiah. They obediently built the walls and re- established Temple worship. Over the next four hundred years the land was inhabited and settled and in so doing set the stage for the birth of Messiah in the Land of Promise mentioned in Micah 5:2:

'But thou, Bethlehem Ephratah, though thou be little among the thousands of Judah, yet out of thee shall he come forth unto me,

that is to be ruler in Israel; whose goings forth have been from of old, from everlasting.'

Daniel also describes this 'One' in clear detail in Chapter 7:13-14.

'I saw in the night visions, and, behold, one like the Son of man came with the clouds of heaven, and came to the Ancient of days, and they brought him near before him.

And there was given him dominion, and glory, and a kingdom, that all people, nations, and languages, should serve him: his dominion is an everlasting dominion, which shall not pass away, and his kingdom that which shall not be destroyed.'

Daniel 7:13-14

The biblical test of a true prophet is if his words come to pass. We know that our Jewish friends balk at the Greek name Jesus, because the 'Christianised' world has sought to systematically destroy Jews in Jesus' name for 2,000 years. However, Jerusalem was destroyed exactly as prophesied by Jesus and the nation was scattered. His word exhorts **all** to clothe the naked, feed the hungry, visit those in prison, give drink to the thirsty and visit the sick; for he said,

'Inasmuch as ye have done it unto one of the least of these *my brethren*, ye have done it unto me.'

Matthew 25:40

Here we are commanded to care for, respect and protect the Jew, along their difficult prophetic pathway.

The Diaspora[1]

Then, for nearly two millenia, the Jews were sent

[1] *The dispersion of the Jews world-wide*

out of the land, as also prophesied by Moses.

'And thou shalt become an astonishment, a proverb, and a byword, among all nations whither the Lord shall lead thee.

And among these nations shalt thou find no ease, neither shall the sole of thy foot have rest: but the Lord shall give thee there a trembling heart, and failing of eyes and sorrow of mind.'

Deuteronomy 28:37, 64, 65

The command, 'bring My sons and My daughters from the ends of the earth,' in Isaiah 45:6, shows us all very plainly that Jews are NOT orphans or heathen, but rather are in the eternal process of being restored as a nation under God.

The Final Home Coming

But the Abrahamic covenant, however, will not allow the Jews to remain scattered forever as mentioned in Jeremiah 31:10.[1]

'Hear the word of the Lord, O ye nations, and declare it in the isles afar off, and say, He that scattered Israel will gather him, and keep him, as a shepherd doth his flock.'

In Isaiah 11:11 and 12, he says the Lord will sovereignly return the people to the land:

[1] *The ingathering of the Jews from throughout the world as discussed more fully in Chapter Seven, entitles "The Gathering of the Exiles".*

'And it shall come to pass in that day, that the Lord shall set His hand again the second time to recover the remnant of His people, which shall be left, from Assyria, and from Egypt, and from from Pathros, and from Cush, *Ethiopia*[1] and from Elam, and from Shinar, and from Hamath, and from the islands of the sea.

And he shall set up an ensign for the nations, and shall assemble the out-casts of Israel, and gather together the dispersed of Judah from the four corners of the earth.'

In chapter thirty, Jeremiah sees Israel and Judah returned to the land, but the price for this final union of land and people is enormous. It will culminate in a world-wide agony and suffering; this will occur when they are once more being established under the sovereign authority of their God. This period of travail of birth is called "Jacob's Trouble" as mentioned in Jeremiah 30:7:

'Alas! For that day is great, so that none is like it: it is even the time of Jacob's trouble; but he shall be saved out of it.'

Believers In The Covenant

Throughout the world today are countless thousands of Christians who choose to stand in support of Israel's right to exist. These are believers who have "crossed over" from darkness into light by faith in the God of Israel. These people represent a mighty force in the world that are doing much to see the Jews reunited with their land, thus fulfilling the eternal Abrahamic Covenant.

God's purposes are clearly presented by Isaiah, Jeremiah, and Ezekiel, not just for Israel but for the Gentile nations as well.

[1] *Author's addition*

'I the Lord have called thee in righteousness, and will hold thine hand, and will keep thee, and give thee for a covenant of the people, for a light of the Gentiles;'

Isaiah 42:6

'Yet the number of the children of Israel shall be as the sand of the sea, which cannot be measured nor numbered; and it shall come to pass, that in the place where it was said unto them, Ye are not my people, there it shall be said unto them, Ye are the sons of the living God.'

Hosea 1:10

'Behold, the days come, saith the Lord, that I will make a new covenant with the house of Israel, and with the house of Judah:

. . . I will put my law in their inward parts, and write it in their hearts; and will be their God, and they shall be my people.

. . . for they shall all know me, from the least of them unto the greatest of them, saith the Lord: for I will forgive their iniquity, and I will remember their sin no more.'

Jeremiah 31:31, 33b, 34b

'I will even gather you from the people, and assemble you out of the countries where ye have been scattered, and I will give you the land of Israel.

And I will give them one heart, and I will put a new spirit with you; and I will take the stoney heart out of their flesh, and will give them an heart of flesh:

. . . and they shall be my people, and I will be their God.'

Ezekiel 11:17,19,20b

[1] *Author's addition*

It is now time for Jews everywhere to discern between the historic, traditionally anti-semetic organization known as the 'church' and believers who adhere to the words of Jesus, and desire to cast their lot in with their spiritual ancestors as forseen by the prophets. Ours is not a conversion campaign, it is rather the ministry of watchman and midwife combined.

"Comfort Ye My People"[1]

The New Testament clearly shows that Christians must act mercifully towards Jews everywhere and thereby release into effect the covenant of God as referred to in Isaiah 59:20,21 and in Romans 11:26-32:

'And so all Israel shall be saved: as it is written, There shall come out of Sion the Deliverer, and shall turn away ungodliness from Jacob:

For this is *my covenant* unto them when I shall take away their sins.

As concerning the gospel, they are enemies for your sakes: but as touching the election, they are beloved for the fathers' sakes.

For the gifts and calling of God are without repentance.

For as ye in times past have not believed God, yet have now obtained mercy through their unbelief:

Even so have these also now not believed, that through *your mercy* they also may *obtain mercy*.

For God hath concluded them all in unbelief, that he might have mercy upon all.'

[1] *Isaiah 40:1.*

This brings us full circle and completes the blessing of "all families of the earth" as prophesied by God to Abraham in Genesis 12:3:

'and in thee shall all families of the earth be blessed.'

Before leaving this section it is of upmost importance to understand something of the forces which have hindered and even forcibly tried to prevent the Jews from "crossing over" and being joined with their land. Numerous examples have been recorded in Bible history and even up to our modern day as evidenced through the **"hunter"**[1] activities of the PLO, Islamic extremists and the Soviet KGB.

The Spirit of Amalek

Going back to the Exodus, the first people who tried to stop the Jews from crossing over the Sinai were the Amalekites. These descendents of Esau exemplified the spirit of anti-semitism. For no apparent reason they attacked the Jews. In the book of Exodus we read that the Amalekites attacked the Israelites in the desert, but in a unique way. They came against the Jews, who were attempting to "cross over" the Sinai Peninsula on their way to receiving the Ten Commandments, the very basis of modern democratic society. The Amelikites came out and for no evident reason, but simply because the refugees were Jewish, attacked them from behind and killed the women and children and weak stragglers. This was the birth of terrorism. The same "modus operendi" is used today in sneak bomb attacks on innocent Israeli civilians, weekly, if not daily, in the city of Jerusalem alone. These attacks do not confront

[1] *Jeremiah 16:16*

military units but attack the defenseless civilians in homes, schools and city centres. This treacherous spirit of Amalek has hounded the Jews down through the centuries through the Egyptians, Syrians, Babylonians, Greeks, Romans, Crusaders, Spanish Inquisitors, the pogroms of Eastern Europe, the Turks, the English mandatory government in Palestine, the Nazis, Islam, the PLO and finally the worldwide Communist system exemplified by the Soviet KGB and their vile propaganda machine against so-called "expansionist Zionism".

The ignominious list is far from complete, but illustrates through history the spirit of Amalek, which attempted to prevent the Jews from coming home and becoming the people God intended them to be. We have the biblical record of the attempts to remove the Jews from their place from Genesis to Malachi. In many instances in the Law and the Prophets we can hear the voices of the giants of the Jewish people speaking out against their sin and anti-semitism, Moses, Joshua, Samuel, David, Isaiah, Jeremiah, Daniel, Mordecai, Esther, Ezekiel, Amos, Zechariah and Jesus. Praise God for biblical history that provides us a lineage of heroism of those that stood up for the preservation of the people of the Book. This record did not end with the ancient prophets of Israel, but continued through the modern revelation of God to man found in the New Testament record, and down to the present hour. Today people who preserved the Jews in the war years of Nazi Europe are known in Israel as "Righteous Gentiles" and have automatic citizenship of Israel.

The Gentile nations have received their entire

spiritual inheritance from the Jewish people. Firstly, the Bible, with its principles of civilisation, then the words of the prophets, and ultimately the Messiah. We must respond in this generation by standing against anti-semitism, first in the Church and then the world. Your local Jews are descendents of your spiritual roots. It is a lie to say you know Jesus and hate the Jews. For Jesus stated very clearly in Matthew 25:40:

'I say unto you, in as much as ye have done it unto one of the least of these my brethren, ye have done it unto me.'

Genesis 12:3 states clearly:

'I will bless them that bless thee, and curse him that curseth thee: and in thee shall all families of the earth be blessed.'

One must always remember that the nation of Israel is the root that bears the branches and Christians were grafted into this tree.

'For if thou wert cut out of the olive tree which is wild by nature, and wert grafted contrary to nature into a good olive tree: how much more shall these, which be the natural branches, be grafted into their own olive tree?'

Romans 11:24

Christians need to take heed for we can be removed if we are high-minded or "conceited"[1] as Paul says. We have not always stood with our brothers, the Jews. But there is no choice, for we are of the same root and in spite of the cost Bible-believers must stand with Israel. If we say that the church is Israel and that God is finished with His ancient people, we are actually cutting off our own roots, which will ultimately lead to death. Corrie

[1] *Romans 11.25*

Ten Boom is a glowing example of a heroine who hid the Jewish people in her attic during the Second World War. She lost many members of her family, including her sister Betsy and her father, to the savage Nazi regime. Her story is preserved in the book and film by the same name, "The Hiding Place". She is but one of many "righteous gentiles".

What is the response of the free world and the Church to the plight of Soviet Jewry? Virtually nothing. Jewish activists in the free world are working to help their brothers, however, the great body of believers who claim adoption into the "commonwealth of Israel"[1] by faith have done very little. Now is the time to act. We will not be guilty by our silence any longer. Here in this volume we have recorded the voices and cries of Jewish people who are still incarcerated in the Soviet Union. Some are in prisons and concentration camps, others are in the prison of daily life in Moscow and Leningrad and throughout the entire Soviet Union.

In reading this information, I trust that you have "crossed over" the barrier of apathy and indifference. This book is a continuation of the voices of those who have cried out down through the centuries of time to preserve the Jewish people.

[1] *Ephesians 2:12*

7

The Gathering Of The Exiles

The relation of the Jews to their land is crucial in understanding God's purposes for them as a nation. The Lord has called them to be an everlasting priesthood throughout their generations and to be an example of service to God among the nations. In fact the purpose of the first exodus is explained when in Exodus the Bible says:

'Then the Lord said unto Moses, Go in unto Pharaoh, and tell him, Thus saith the Lord God of the Hebrews, Let my people go, that they may serve me.'[1]

Could this be indicative of the purposes behind the final "exodus" of the Jews from the land of the North?

In observing the history of the Jewish people and their relation to the land as a nation there have been three dispersions and two ingatherings, the first being the sojourn in Egypt, the second dispersion partly to Babylon and to the areas north of Israel. Some Bible scholars claim that this was not a complete national dispersion and that the second was when the Temple was destroyed in 70 AD and the Jews were scattered throughout the

[1] *Exodus 9:1*

world. When the Bible says in Isaiah 11:11 and 12

'I will gather them a *second* time'

this must refer to the current ingathering of the Jewish people which began over the last one hundred years or so.

The modern ingathering of the nation of Israel to their physical homeland has been nothing short of miraculous. This subject is a book in itself, however, it is important to show that the scriptures clearly say that this final ingathering will be from the four corners of the earth. Isaiah 43:5-7 says,

'Fear not, for I am with thee: I will bring thy seed from the *east*, and gather thee from the *west*;

I will say to the *north*, Give up: and to the *south*, Keep not back: bring my sons from far and my daughters from the ends of the earth; even every one that is called by my name: for I have created him for my glory, I have formed him; yea, I have made him.'

Waves of Aliyah

In the last century there have been a series of cycles of immigration into the land of Israel from all over the world, called "Waves of Aliyah". Aliyah means to "go up to the land". Since the destruction of the Second Temple in Jerusalem in 70 AD and up until the 1880's the Jewish population of Israel fluctuated between several thousand to sometimes more than 25,000. However, between the 1880's and 1930 the first waves of the modern return to the land of Israel began, laying the foundations for the establishment of the State of Israel. This movement of Jewish people to the land was caused by the following facts: the ancient, everlasting covenants of God, the age-old devotion of the Jews to their historic homeland and hope of messianic redemption, the intensification of anti- semitism against the Jewish communities in Eastern Europe and Czarist Russia, and Muslim lands, and the efforts of an active minority who believed that the only lasting and fundamental solution to the Jewish problem was in the return to Israel.[1]

By 1897 and the advent of Theodore Herzl and the beginning of the World Zionist Organisation in Basle, the concept of a Jewish state was slowly growing in the minds of Jewish people worldwide. The way ahead, however, was to be very rocky. By 1903 and the end of the "first wave" of aliyah some 10,000 immigrant Jews had settled the country in agricultural settlements while 3,000 newcomers had established homes in Jaffa which gave the early beginning to the urbanization of Tel Aviv. After the death of Herzl in 1904 and a slowdown of Zionist fervour, new pogroms in Kishinev, Russia rekindled the impetus for a fresh wave of aliyah. This second wave was also spurred on by the Zionist-Socialist ideals of Russian Jews influenced by Marxist thinking. Thus physical labour replaced organisational discussions and the "Ha Halutzim" or pioneer movement gathered momentum. This, coupled with the financial help offered by the newly-formed Jewish National Fund, and the beginnings of a Jewish self- defence organisation, called "Ha Shomer", plus the establishment of the Kibbutz Movement and the introduction of Hebrew into all spheres of life, brought the numbers of settlers up to 85,000 by 1914. This new and strong group of Jewish pioneers acted like a magnet to draw others to the land. World War One

[1] *Israel Pocket Library, "Immigration and Settlement", Keter Publishing Company, Jerusalem, Israel, 1973, page 13.*

interrupted the influx to Israel, but by 1917 and the assurance of the Balfour Declaration a Jewish homeland was guaranteed by British decree. This gave new hope in spite of the resurgence of horrific anti-semitic excesses in the Ukraine, Poland and Hungary. This, in fact, brought more settlers. However, the British mandatory government under Arab pressure began to enforce the beginning of a quota system on the number of Jewish immigrants allowed into Palestine.

Simultaneously, in 1917 revolutionary Russia closed its gates to the world and effectively sealed off three million Jews. However, the participants in the 'Third Wave' of aliyah from 1919 to 1923 began to play a key role in developing the infrastructure of what would later become Israel, by providing roads, housing and the beginnings of industry to strengthen the fledgling economy. From then until the mid-thirties the influx of people continued gradually. However, with the shadow of Nazism being cast over Western civilisation, the number of Jewish refugees began to increase alarmingly. This, coupled with the quota system, began to create an anomalous situation of thousands of refugees with nowhere to go.

In 1936 Dr. Chaim Weizmann said in regard to the Jews that "the world was divided into places where they cannot live and places where they cannot enter". The only place of refuge for the refugees was Palestine, the place of Divine choice. By 1938 the sufferings inflicted on the German Jews by the Nazi regime attracted worldwide attention. In that year President Roosevelt called an international conference in Evian, France, to seek homes for the refugees. The dismal failure of the conference, which was not allowed to even consider Palestine, showed that no-one was ready to welcome Jewish refugees except the yishuv or the community of Jewish people in Palestine. By 1937, due to Arab pressure, the British issued their infamous "White Paper" which absolutely limited Jewish immigration and even proposed that further Jewish immigration at the end of five years would be dependent on Arab consent. This White Paper was denounced by many non-Jewish sympathisers as a betrayal of Britain's obligations under the mandate. This created the illegal immigration movement and more and more refugee ships made their way to Palestine.[1]

As a Canadian, I am ashamed to point out that at this time Canada closed its gates to the enormous number of refugees created by Hitler's "final solution" regime. A senior Canadian immigration official in 1945 was asked how many Jews would be allowed into Canada after the War, "none", he said, "is too many."[2] His reponse seems to reflect the prevailing view of a substantial number of his fellow citizens. May this never happen again. It is documented fact that the few German Jewish professors and others who were able to get into Canada during the war came in disguised as Protestants. May this atrocity of human justice never happen again. This is one reason for this book and film by the same title. My prayer is that we in the West will not be complacent while our Jewish friends in the Soviet Union are experiencing a re-enactment of history.

[1] *Israel Pocket Library. Immigration and Settlement. page 26.*
[2] *Abella, Irving and Troper, Harold, "None Is Too Many", Lester and Orpen, Denny's, Toronto, Canada, 1982, page 9, ix.*

Ingathering

In 1945 the world was shocked and ashamed at the realisation of the extent of the Nazi hatred and evil perpetrated against the Jewish people. Six million or one third of the entire Jewish population had been tortured and slaughtered in this satanic plot we have come to call the Holocaust.[1] This was one of the most barbaric attempts by Man to circumvent the Abrahamic Covenant given 4,000 years before linking God, the Jews and their land.

Fortunately, the Divine principle of life coming from death was still in operation. For out of the death camps of Nazism came the miraculous birth of the Zionist ideal, the State of Israel. On May 14 1948, David Ben Gurion and his cabinet declared the creation of the State of Israel, fulfilling Isaiah's prophecy that a nation would be born in a day.[2] Within fifteen minutes the provisional government of Israel was recognised by the United States of America under President Harry S. Truman. The supernatural flow of history was overriding the natural. The covenants of God were still shaping the history of mankind. The Israeli Declaration of Independence proclaimed that the State of Israel would be open to Jewish immigration and the ingathering of the exiles. The first Provisional Council decision was to abolish all restrictions on immigration. The Law of Return and Citizenship Law of 1952 grants every Jew who so chooses an instant and automatic right to settle in Israel as a citizen. Whereas in the diaspora the Jews were a people without a country, at the time of their return to Israel the land was without a people. This was to

[1] *Means "burnt sacrifice"*

[2] *Isaiah 66:8*

change rapidly, as the people and the land were finally united and continues to this day. In 1984, 20,000 refugees were absorbed, including thousands of Ethiopian Jews.

Since the beginning of statehood the Jewish population has grown more than sixfold, from 650,000 in 1948 to nearly four million in 1985; almost half of the increase has come from aliyah which totals 1,700,000. Our personal efforts to encourage Jews worldwide to come to Israel from 1970 to 1982 are recorded in our book entitled "Fishers and Hunters". It is important to note that the ingathering of the exiles has been from the East, West, South and North.

'Fear not: for I am with thee: I will bring thy seed from the east, and gather thee from the west;

I will say to the north Give up; and to the south, Keep not back: bring my sons from far, and my daughters from the ends of the earth;

Isaiah 43:5,6

From The East

Iraq

Entire Jewish communities have come from several Arab countries at considerable cost. In 1950 the Iraqi government enacted a law authorising Jewish departure, however, all property had to be left behind. Of Iraq's 130,000 Jews, 121,500 did not hesitate and over a period of eight months the aerial "Operation Ezra and Nehemiah" brought them to sanctuary in their homeland. By 1961 184,130 Israelis were registered as being of Iraqi origin.

Syria

The situation in Syria is a disturbing one as more than 4,500 Syrian Jews have been forbidden to leave a country characterised by instability and revolution. Despite the announcement in late 1976 that some restrictions had been lifted, Syria's Jews are still denied the right to leave, while other basic human freedoms are also withheld.

Iran

In 1961 there were more than 61,000 Jews of Iranian origin in Israel and out of that number 37,000 Persian speaking. Since 1979 and the takeover of Iran by the Ayatollah Khomeini and the severing of diplomatic relations with Israel, most of the remaining Iranian Jews have made their way to Israel. A few still remain and they are in great danger.

India

Most of India's 20,000 Jews arrived in Israel after 1948. A few still remain in Bombay and Cochin.

China

'Behold, these shall come from far: and, lo, these from the north and from the west; and these from the land of Sinim.'

Isaiah 49:12

Sinim is the Hebrew word for China. Following the Communist Chinese takeover in 1949 the vast majority of China's Jewish population left. By 1951 2,167 Jews had arrived in Israel while the others were scattered throughout the world, some to Hong Kong, Singapore, Tokyo and Seoul. Today there are only several hundred Jews in Kaifeng[1]

[1] *Ackman, David, "New Hope For China's Jews", Time Magazine, February 11th, 1985.*

and interestingly in spite of nearly complete assimilation they still avoid eating pork and have a history of attempting to observe Passover. Currently the task of building a Jewish Museum and perhaps even a synagogue in east central China with government sanction heralds a new day for the Jews of Sinim and speaks of involvement in their preservation.

From The West

The gathering of the exiles from the Western nations has been in two major phases. During the first period from 1880 to 1967 immigrants arrived from Eastern and Central Europe due to the "push" of their respective countries' anti-semitic attitudes. This was true in countries such as Poland, Germany, Hungary, Rumania, Czechoslovakia, Yugoslavia and Bulgaria.

After the Six-Day War, however, significant aliyah began from Western Europe, North and Latin America and the British Commonwealth. Aliyah from these Western countries was largely a result of the "pull" from the Israeli society rather than the push from a hostile and oppressive environment. Sadly, this has tapered off during the last fifteen years. In 1971 8,122 immigrants came from North America while in 1980 only 2,493 arrived.

From The South

Yemen

'Ye have seen what I did unto the Egyptians, and how I bare you on eagles' wings, and brought you unto myself.'

Exodus 19:4

The ingathering of Jews from areas south of Israel has been very interesting. In 1949 virtually all of Yemen's Jewry were airlifted to Israel on "Operation Magic Carpet". A unique part of their story relates to the fact that their repatriation program was facilitated because of their knowledge of Holy Scriptures. When asked if they were frightened to fly to Israel in an airplane, since many of them were simple nomadic desert people, they replied emphatically, "No!". They were confident when they saw the American eagle painted on the side of the airplanes that they would be "borne up to Zion on eagles wings"! They also knew in 1949 that there was a King David ruling in Israel once again. He was, of course, Prime Minister David Ben Gurion.

Africa

In some countries of North Africa almost the entire Jewish community has left for Israel. One notable exception is Algeria were most of the population of 130,000 Jews went to settle in France. However, a total of 414,201 have come from African nations between 1948 and 1980, including the entire Egyptian community.

Ethiopia

One of the most wonderful emigrations of Jewish populations is the recent miracle "Operation Moses" homecoming of the "Beta-Israel", a portion of the Jewish population of Ethiopia. Their origins are still shrouded in mystery but they have maintained their cultural and religious ethniticity in spite of huge obstacles. They were discovered in the 18th century by the Nile explorer James Bruce. Through the ages they have survived extreme hardships, inter-tribal conflict, war, persecution, alienation, starvation, disease and drought.

In 1975 Israeli Shephardi Chief Rabbi Ovadia Yosef ruled that they were members of the lost tribe of Dan and therefore entitled to Israeli citizenship under the "Law of Return". No major effort was made to bring Ethiopian Jews to Israel over the years and up until recently only about 300 had made their way to Israel. When Menachem Begin became Prime Minister in 1977 he resolved to bring the Ethiopian Jews to Israel, but after two plane loads arrived the operation was aborted by a "slip of the tongue" by the then Foreign Minister, Moshe Dayan. The immigration effort was renewed several years ago, and in recent months it was speeded up by Prime Minister Shimon Peres and his predecessor Yitzak Shamir. "The Ethiopian Jews believe they have been delivered from a land of famine and pestilence and returned to their ancestral homeland. They see it in terms of a miracle on the road to Redemption, and an answer to prayers they have recited for thousands of years in exile. But there is great sorrow for the countless thousands who have died of disease and starvation, and consternation over the fact that the story of the operation has been revealed before all of the Ethiopian Jews are safe in Israel."[1]

The exhortation of the scripture concerning the Jews of "the South" in Isaiah 43:6 says,

'I will say to the South, Keep not back: bring my sons from far, and my daughters from the ends of the earth;'

"We understand that our efforts for the release of all Ethiopian Jews must be employed in prayer and quiet action until the remaining 18,000 Ethiopian Jews are home."[1]

[1] *Rappaport-Louis, Jerusalem Post, January 6th, 1985.*

South Africa

One of the most wealthy and affluent Jewish communities in the world has continually sent immigrants to Israel. By 1972 some 8,097 South Africans had come from the south, "held not back" by the comfort and ease of their surroundings.

South America

There has never been a large immigration movement from South America but between 1971 and 1980 30,574 Jews have come from Latin American countries.

From The North

'I will say to the North, 'Give up!'

Isaiah 43:6

'Therefore, behold, the days come, saith the Lord, that it shall no more be said, The Lord liveth, that brought up the children of Israel out of the land of Egypt;

But, The Lord liveth, that brought up the children of Israel from the land of the north, and from all the lands whither he had driven them: and I will bring them again into their land that I gave unto their fathers.'

Jeremiah 16:14-16

The scriptures clearly speak of a huge "exodus" of Jews from the land of the north. This will even eclipse the first exodus from Egypt. Since October 1968 to December 1984 some 264,517 Jews left the Soviet Union, commonly regarded as the land of the north by Bible scholars. In spite of the fact that not all of the Jews came to Israel, this total figure represents approximately 10% of the entire Jewish population in the USSR. The question arises, does the Lord fulfill his prophetic word completely or only to 10%? I believe that He fulfills his promises 100% and a growing number of Christians in the world, particularly in Scandinavia and Western Europe and North America attest to this. They have expressed their faith in the release of a large number of Soviet Jews by massive preparations to assist them as they will pass through their respective countries on their way to Israel. The size of the response has been phenomenal and is clearly documented in Steve Lightle's book, "Exodus II"[1], in which Steve recounts how several years ago, while in a long season of prayer, he saw in a vision a mass exit of Jews from Russia. This was so extraordinary that he hardly spoke about it for six years. Then, during the last several years in his travels to Scandinavia he began to hear reports of Christian believers who were getting the same message from the Holy Spirit and that they were making preparations to help the Russian Jews with food, clothing, lodging and transportation on their way to Zion. The Bible says that the Lord won't do anything unless He first shows it to His prophets.

'Surely the Lord God will do nothing, but he revealeth his secret unto his servants the prophets.'
Amos 3:7

We believe in this vision of a mass exodus of Soviet Jews, for our personal involvement with Soviet Jewry began in 1972. However, we also believe that in the free world we are obligated now to help the Jews inside Russia who are undergoing extreme hardship and persecution. Giving a voice to Russian Jewry today is the objective of our film and book, "Gates of Brass". This task is directly

[1] *Hunter Books, U.S.A.* *Bridge Publishing, U.K.*

linked to the unfolding fulfilment of Bible prophecy and the coming of Messiah.

In the marvellous 45th chapter of the Book of Isaiah concerning the salvation of Israel, the Lord says that God and Man will have a part in the release of the captives from the Soviet Union.

'Thus saith the Lord, the Holy One of Israel, and his Maker, Ask me of things to come concerning my sons, and concerning the work of my hands command ye me.

I have made the earth, and created man upon it: I, even my hands, have stretched out the heavens, and all their host (army) have I commanded.

I have raised him up in righteousness, and I will direct all his ways: he shall build my city, and he SHALL LET GO MY CAPTIVES, not for price nor reward, saith the Lord of Hosts.'

Isaiah 45:11-13

Some people scoff at this literal belief in the Word of God for they cannot see it. They are in a way blind. But the Lord and His ways, indeed His strategies are often hidden from the proud and lofty.

'Verily thou art a God that hidest thyself, O God of Israel, the Saviour.'

Isaiah 45:15

The ingathering of the ancient exiles of Israel worldwide is directly related to the redemption of Israel and to the appearance of the Messiah.

'But Israel shall be saved in the Lord with an everlasting salvation: ye shall not be ashamed nor confounded world without end.'

Isaiah 45:17

'When the Lord shall build up Zion, He shall

appear in his glory.'

Psalm 102:6

Thus the building up of Zion is a distinct sign of the soon coming of Messiah. In this very next passage of scripture it is evident that this ingathering will involve prisoners and those prevented by Man from returning to Zion.

'For he hath looked down from the height of his sanctuary; from heaven did the Lord behold the earth;

To hear the groaning of the prisoner; to lose those that are appointed to death;'

Psalm 102:19

'See, I will bring them from the land of the north and gather them from the ends of the earth.'

Jeremiah 31:8

'They will return from the land of the enemy.'

Jeremiah 31:11

So there is hope for your future, declares the Lord in Jeremiah 31:17.

'Thus saith the Lord of hosts; The children of Israel and the children of Judah were oppressed together: and all that took them captives held them fast; they refused to let them go.

Their Redeemer is strong; the Lord of hosts is his name: He shall thoroughly plead their cause, that he may give rest to the land.'

Jeremiah 50:33,34

'For it shall come to pass in that day, saith

the Lord of hosts, that I will break his yoke off thy neck, and will burst thy bonds, and strangers shall no more serve themselves of him:

But they shall serve the Lord their God, and David their king, whom I will raise unto them.

Therefore fear thou not, O my servant Jacob, saith the Lord; neither be dismayed, O Israel: for, lo, I will SAVE thee from afar, and thy seed from the land of their captivity; and Jacob shall return, and shall be in rest, and be quiet, and none shall make him afraid.'

Jeremiah 30:8-11

'Thus saith the Lord God, Behold, I will lift up mine hand to the Gentiles, and set up my standard to the people: and they shall bring thy sons in their arms, and thy daughters shall be carried upon their shoulders.'

Isaiah 49:22

There is a direct relation in scripture to the release, return, restoration and revival of God's chosen people and the ultimate redemption of mankind. From the above scriptures it is evident that the Lord is directly involved in the release and return of His people from the nations of the world and especially from the land of the north where they are held in captivity. The restoration of the Jewish people to the land of Israel has already happened in part, activating the Abrahamic covenant to culminate in the salvation of the nation of Israel.

'For I will take you from among the nations, and gather you out of all countries, and will bring you into your own land.

Then will I sprinkle clean water upon you,

and ye shall be clean ; from all your filthiness, and from all your idols, will I cleanse you.

A new heart also will I give you, and a new spirit will I put within you: and I will take away the stony heart out of your flesh, and I will give you a heart of flesh.

And I will put my spirit within you, and cause you to walk in my statutes, and ye shall keep my judgements, and do them.

And ye shall dwell in the land that I gave to your fathers; and ye shall be my people, and I will be your God.'

Ezekiel 36:24-28

'One shall say, I am the Lord's; and another shall call himself by the name of Jacob; and another shall subscribe with his hand unto the Lord, and surname himself by the name of Israel.'

Isaiah 44:5

'Behold, the days come, saith the Lord, that I will make a new covenant with the house of Israel, and with the house of Judah, not according to the covenant that I made with their fathers in the day that I took them by the hand to bring them out of the land of Egypt, which, my covenant, they broke, although I was an husband unto them, saith the Lord;

But this shall be the covenant that I will make with the house of Israel: After those days, saith the Lord, I will put my law in their inward parts, and will write it in their hearts, and will be their God, and they shall be my people.

And they shall teach no more every man his neighbour, and every man his brother, saying,

know the Lord; for they shall all know me, from the least of them unto the greatest of them, saith the Lord; for I will forgive their iniquity, and I will remember their sin no more.'

Jeremiah 31:31-34

The Word of God clearly speaks of the final restoration of Jews to the "land of promise" and the resultant outpouring of the Spirit of God upon them bringing national revival and ultimately world revival.

'And it shall come to pass afterward, that I will pour out my Spirit upon all flesh; and your sons and your daughters shall prophesy, your old men shall dream dreams, your young men shall see visions:

And also upon the servants and upon the handmaids in those days will I pour out my Spirit.'

Joel 2:28,29

'And I will gather the remnant of my flock out of all countries whither I have driven them, and will bring them again to their folds; and they shall be fruitful and increase.

And I will set up shepherds over them which shall feed them: and they shall fear no more, nor be dismayed, neither shall they be lacking, saith the Lord.

Behold, the days come, saith the Lord, that I will raise unto David a righteous Branch, and a king shall reign and prosper, and shall execute judgement and justice in the earth.'

Jeremiah 23:3-5

This is a distinct reference to the Messiah of

Israel and is confirmed by this scripture in Isaiah.

'Look unto me, and be ye saved, all the ends of the earth: for I am God and there is none else.

I have sworn by myself, the word is gone out of my mouth in righteousness, and shall not return.

That unto me every knee shall bow, and every tongue shall swear.

In the Lord shall all the seed of Israel be justified, and shall glory.'

Isaiah 45:22,23,25

'In his days Judah shall be saved, and Israel shall dwell safely: and this is his name whereby he shall be called, THE LORD OUR RIGHTEOUSNESS.

Therefore, behold, the days come, saith the Lord, that shall no more say, The Lord liveth, which brought up the children of Israel out of the land of Egypt;

But, the Lord liveth, which brought up and which led the seed of the house of Israel out of the north country, and from the countries whither I had driven them; and they shall dwell in their own land.'

Jeremiah 23:6,7,8

The full revelation of the meaning of this scripture is indeed profound for the Jewish people worldwide and particularly in Israel.

8

The Heroes

My life was changed when I met the Jews in the Soviet Union. Meridel, our 12-year-old son Chris, and I went to visit them during Passover 1983. We represented thousands of Christians worldwide who were fasting and praying for them during the Esther Fast. We went to encourage them that the Bible mentions them specifically, stating that they are going to be released in a mass exodus that will eclipse the exodus from Egypt in magnitude and world influence.

' "The days are coming," declares the Lord, "when I will raise up to David a righteous Branch, a King who will reign wisely and do what is just and right in the land.

"In his days Judah will be saved and Israel will live in safety. This is the name by which he will be called: The Lord Our Righteousness.

"So then the days are coming," declares the Lord, "when people will no longer say, 'as surely as the Lord lives, who brought the Israelites up out of Egypt,' but they will say, 'As surely as the Lord lives, who brought the descendants of Israel up out of the land of the

north and out of all the countries where he had banished them,' then they will live in their own land." '

Jeremiah 23:5-8 NIV

We couldn't help but be blessed and challenged by their courage and grit. They were not bitter. They did not speak evil of the Soviet Union; all they wanted was their freedom. They were noble in their attitudes and had not lost their sense of humour. Their 'spirit' and example of perseverance and faith after years of unjustified persecution made me wonder how I would endure in a similar situation. I began to see the Scripture of Isaiah 45:3 in a new light:

'I will give you the treasures of darkness, riches stored in secret places, so that they may know that I am the Lord, the God of Israel, who calls you by name.'

These Jewish people were living treasures and their lives shone like hidden riches in dark places. Ease and luxury cannot produce the polished saints that are found in places like China and Russia. They have paid the price for their faith; and in spite of an imprisoned existence they are free people.

As you read their statements, please remember that it has cost them everything to speak the truth. The Soviet authorities are striving to silence their voices. One of the official Russian newspapers printed the following in regard to our type of activity:

'Tourists to Russia from the West are actually Zionist emissaries with instructions for renegades. These renegades or Jewish activists had agreed to supply the Zionist agents with slanderous materials or fabrications against the USSR.'

The following activities are considered to be anti-Soviet:[1]

- Lecturing on Jewish history and Judaism.
- Studying the Torah (Bible) in small groups.
- Holding concerts of Jewish songs.
- Performances of Jewish amateur theatre.
- Providing walking tours of "historical" Jewish sites in Leningrad.
- Celebrating Jewish holidays and Sabbaths.
- Studying Hebrew.

Now read the statements transcribed from filmed interviews smuggled out of Russia after our second visit to these "dangerous" people.

Ya'acov Gorodetsky

Ya'acov has championed the cause of Jewish rights in Leningrad. In January 1983, after many intimidating warnings and beatings by the KGB, he was fired from his job as a teacher in an evening insitute for adults.

'There are about two million Jews in the USSR, but for the vast majority of them, everything Jewish consists only of the vexing mark **Jewish** on the nationality line in their passport and in other bureaucratic questionnaires. Hundreds of thousands of Jews here know nothing about Jewish history, culture, or Jewish language. And this is not surprising because they have practically no opportunity to do so. Hence recently one can learn the most about Jewishness and Jews from anti-Zionist broadcasts and publications.

The KGB will physically beat us, but will they put us in jail? I have earned my strength during six

[1] ***Pravda**, 23 October 1982.*

years of my refusal . . . But you must know: It is a very hard situation for us, considerably harder than two or three years ago. Please, remember this when you wish to be angry with us . . .'

Natasha Khassina

Natasha and her husband, a maths professor, and their two daughters live in Moscow. They have repeatedly applied to emigrate to Israel in spite of mounting difficulties originating from the KGB. Natasha has been classified as a 'permanent refusenik' who will never be allowed to leave the USSR. In spite of this she has taken on the task of helping Prisoners of Zion during increasingly difficult times.

'We applied for an exit visa in 1976 and received a refusal on grounds of so-called security considerations. The OVIR[1] declared that my departure threatens the security of 260 million Soviet citizens. But such a reason is not substantiated to stop our departure and also the departure of hundreds and perhaps even thousands of families who have received a refusal for the same reason. The fact is I left my profession connected with secrecy considerations 15 years ago. Clearly during this time information has been updated to such an extent that the knowledge which we had does not represent any kind of security risk.

At present this pretext for refusal on grounds of secrecy is used only as a pretext not to give us an exit visa. On numerous occasions we appealed to the Ministry of Foreign Affairs which deals directly with visas; but we were unable to have our case genuinely reviewed.

[1] *Visa Office*

Hundreds of thousands of families continue to this day to wait for exit visas. We have no hope that this situation will improve. The authorities say that we should not leave the Soviet Union because we were born and grew up here. In fact we wish that at least our children will be able to grow up and live in Israel and not in the Soviet Union.'

Alex Zelichenok

'I am 47 years old and live in Leningrad. I have been a refusenik since 1978. What can be said about the past years? It seems that they were much longer than 7½ years and so empty it feels like 15 years have passed. So many things have happened during this time – both tragic and sad; something like a farce or "theatre of the absurd." The essence of a refusenik's life is not in events, even the most tragic ones. This life is not like anything else.

I would like to be an optimist; but to my sorrow there is no basis – not even a hint of a positive development. And as to negative signs – they are in great quantity. I think that soon all these difficulties will demand additional strength from us.

It is difficult to explain our lives to a person who has not lived here or been born here. Even a prisoner knows the length of his prison term and when he will be freed. We know nothing. Even a hostage seized by terrorists or pirates knows the conditions for his release or the amount of ransom which must be paid for him. No conditions for release have been determined for us. A person in this condition cannot plan his life beyond tomorrow. And even such short-term planning turns out to be unsound. No human psyche, even the psyche of very strong people, can bear this terrible burden.

I shall tell only about a search which happened to me two years ago. The KGB showed me a search warrant which ordered the removal of printed material allegedly in my possession of a slanderous nature defaming the Soviet order. Of course I didn't have such material. Nevertheless, they took away over 40 books.

What kind of books were these? For example they took away a book of Arthur Conan Doyle and English language textbooks printed in Poland. Almost all of my books were in Hebrew and they confiscated the following: A children's book; a songbook in Hebrew; a table of verb conjugations; a grammar book; some dictionaries; the newspaper **Shaar le-matkhil**[1]. For two years I have been fighting to have them returned to me . . .

And, nevertheless, we remain optimists and believe in a better future. We believe that we shall be in Israel. On what is our faith based? Perhaps so that you will understand, I shall relate one incident.

Recently a search occurred in Odessa involving a young family of refuseniks. A teenage girl was lying sick in the room. She had just returned from the hospital and was convalescing from a heart operation. She watched them take away all the family's Hebrew books. But one remained. She lay immobile, hiding it under her nightgown.

If you will think about this, you will understand what our faith is based on. We believe: **"Am Yisrael Chai!"** – The nation of Israel lives. We shall overcome some day!'

[1] *Paper in elementary Hebrew for beginners.*

Yosef Radomysl'sky

Yosef lives in Leningrad and was permanently or eternally refused an exit visa to Israel in January 1982. He gave this interview in Hebrew.

'I am a reusenik and also a teacher of Hebrew. These are my two professions. Indeed, I have one other profession; I am an engineer, but since my refusal I have not worked as an engineer.

'I am very happy to have the opportunity to send greetings to my friends in Israel and throughout the entire world. Thanks to your support and help we feel that we are not alone in the world. This is the most important thing for us now when the situation is getting worse.

One of our friends, Yosef Begun, has been sentenced for 12 years for teaching Hebrew. This is especially important now when another friend of ours, Lev Elbert, awaits his terrible fate in prison.

Now many Jews want – even yearn – to depart from here, to make aliyah to Israel; and the number of refuseniks continues to increase. This displeases the authorities and they try to decrease our number. They don't even permit us to deliver our documents to the OVIR visa office and this is their way of decreasing the number of refuseniks here.

Other signs that the situation is worsening are found in Soviet propaganda books, material in the press, and movies which tell the Russian people that during World War II the Jews helped the Nazis to get ready for the war and falsified all the history of the war. You can imagine the effect since Russian people suffered a lot during the Second World War when over 20 million died.'

Grigory Wasserman

Address: USSR
195276 Leningrad
Prospekt Kultury
27 1 89

Grigory, an observant Jew, was born in 1950. He was trained professionally as a radio engineer. He was refused an exit visa to Israel in 1978 and since that time he has been working an an elevator mechanic. He is a Hebrew teacher and lecturer on Jewish history and Judaism. Furthermore, he is one of two men who founded regular Jewish seminars in Leningrad and is one of the most respected spritual leaders among Soviet Jews.

In December 1982 he was called into the OVIR visa office and told that his refusal was final and permanent and that he had no right to apply ever again for an exit visa to Israel.

Grigory spoke in Hebrew for this interview which was filmed in Leningrad:

'First of all I want to say a few words about the spiritual condition of the Jews of Russia. Generally they are sick people, and this disease has a name: materialism. This is a fundamental disease and all the rest is just a consequence of this condition which leads to assimilation and **neshir** or dropping out. When a man is sick, he doesn't go to an engineer, nor to an electrician, nor to a chemist. He goes to a doctor, to an expert. And this is something that we need very much now. We need expertise in the matter of helping Russian Jews.

Enough of empty declarations, enough of words, enough of amateur activities. We need only expertise. If not, it will be too late. Perhaps it is already a bit too late in order to help and save all two million that remain here.

There is a great need now because emigration has stopped. We must examine and search again for new approaches to see how and in what way to help. In spite of total depression and despair, in spite of the darkest atmosphere and more than hopeless future, I have succeeded to overcome.

However you must know that I am not a man with an iron will. I am human! Now the time is hard; it is bad for everyone and for some of us it is especially difficult.

I am glad that I have seen Lev Elbert. He is a very, very good man. Together with Yaelena Dubianskaya we have spent two days in stimulating, realistic discussion.

. . . Our situation reminds me of a large battleground. There are many dead; heaps of bodies are still stirring and groans are heard. Very few are still alive and they could be saved. This is our work.'

Evgeny Lein

Address: USSR
194356 Leningrad
Prospekt Engelsa 135-21
Lein, Evgeny
Telephone: 5178562

Evgeny Lein is one of the most brilliant, disciplined and gentle-mannered refuseniks I met. He was born in 1939 and graduated from Leningrad University in 1963, receiving a Ph.D. in the field of systems programming and systems control. He is the author of 20 scientific publications.

His wife, Soboleva Irina, was born in 1939 and graduated from Leningrad University in 1963 with a Ph.D. in the field of biochemistry. She is the author of 15 scientific publications.

Their daughter, Alexandra Nehama Lein, was born in 1960; and their son, Alexei, was born in 1971.

During July 1978 the family applied for a visa to Israel and in September 1978 they were refused in spite of the fact that neither Evgeny nor Irina had any connection with classified information. After their application, Evgeny and Irina were forced to "retire" from their jobs. On April 14 1980 Alexandra was brutally beaten up in the street by "persons unknown"; and on October 23 1982 Evgeny was called "the constant criminal" in an article entitled "uninvited guests" by A. Kostrov, published in the central newspaper **Izvestia**.

'Seven years ago I first turned to the Soviet government with a request to leave for Israel, but I received a refusal. By profession I am a mathematician; but I was fired on the same day that I requested a visa for Israel. My wife, a chemist, also lost her work. My daughter was dismissed from her institute.

On May 18 1981 I was arrested at a lecture on the history of Jewish culture which took place at my friend's apartment. When the lecture began, the door suddenly opened and a large group of policemen and people in 'civies' burst into the apartment. The lecture was broken up and I was arrested on the charge of striking a policeman.

I didn't do this and many of the witnesses corroborated my innocence; but I was immediately arrested and put in the former Czarist prison of Kresty, where I was held, together with hardened criminals. There were eight inmates in a room which was seven metres square. There was no daylight in the room and I spent months in it under round-the-clock electric lighting.

A continual sensation of hunger and repeated threats of physical reprisal hung over me. The prosecutor deprived me not only of the right to letters, but also of a meeting with a lawyer. I was condemned in order to intimidate my friends who are refuseniks. I knew this. I spent 6½ months in prison and 6 months in Siberia.

After my return to Leningrad I was unable to find work. And then, according to the directive of the Executive Committee, I was sent to work as a stoker or operator of a gas boiler.

I am a mathematician by profession but my wages consisted of only 60 rubles. For comparison, I pay 50 rubles a month for my apartment. This salary is a ridiculous sum which is below the official minimum subsistence level.

I declare that neither a new threat of judicial persecution nor difficulties will force us to change our decision. We believe we shall succeed in departing for Israel. I thank you.'

Recently news has reached up that following an afternoon visit with tourists from the West, Evgeny was attacked by KGB agents in the entrance to his apartment. They beat him severely on the ears (he is deaf in one ear), and while he was on the ground, they stepped on his right hand breaking his fingers. It was reported that one of the agents said, "The next time you apply to go to Israel, you will have to do it with your left hand".

Boris Klotz – Moscow

'I have been a refusenik for five years; and in my experience those unpleasantries and problems which I have confronted have arisen since my application to go to Israel. Therefore, I want to tell about what led me to this step, about the reasons which forced us to make this decision.

I must say that the very understanding of those reasons changed during the five years which I have spent as a refusenik. At the beginning it seemed like the hard external aspects of our life were the main reasons for our application to leave; but with the passing of these years, it seems to me that I can now look into the spiritual roots of my decision. Now I can formulate it in the following words.

My desire to participate in history is possible only through the nation of Israel. For me participation in history is possible only through my Jewishness. This self-identification as a Jew leads me into our historical circle. When I compare my views and my life five years ago, it is as if I have climbed to a high mountain peak and I see a vast panorama extending far around. Of course this ascent demanded many efforts – it was difficult; but that view which has opened up is undoubtedly worth many sacrifices.

Precisely because of such an attitude to our place in history, all our vision, even in spite of our practical problems, focuses on this issue of Jewish emigration and the return to our land. My strivings, the future of my children and my family, the future of our nation, our culture, focus on our State – Israel. In this sense, it is possible to say that our aliya – movement upwards – has already begun. Therefore in such an understanding, this is not only a geographical and physical displacement, this is also a spiritual movement. We already sense it.

But like any movement it demands everything and is undoubtedly connected with great costs. When I think about that, then I feel that I made the right choice. On the other hand, I want my children to follow me; but when I think of what sacrifices they might have to bear on this pathway, then I feel terrible.'

Psalm

O Lord, I sing Thy praise
In the turmoil and darkness
Of the heathen temple.
Thou art, O Lord, indescribable,
Incomparable, invisible, omnipresent . . .
And here am I who speak of meaning,
The meaning of my life in this world.
Mine is the right to decide,
Choice and action.
Thou art word and meaning,
Thou the observer.

I love Thy grass O Lord,
The sun and petitions in the night.
The woman whom I have yet to meet,
The book I have yet to write.
I love the fragrance, the sounds, the colours,
Of flowers, of the sea, of birds, of freedom.
But still more I love meaning:
That the tree may grow from the earth,
Man from boy
And word from truth.
The meaning of the sweet wine,
The salt sea,

The bitter cloud,
But not the sweet lie
And bitter freedom.

I have learned to see sweetness
In barbed wire thorns,
In Ural snows,
In smiling prison guards.
I have understood that even a
Four-month fast may be sweet,
Without wine, without the sea.

In the smells, sounds, sights
Of the Concentration Camp
I have felt and understood
The sweetness of freedom.
Thy word, truth, meaning, and I myself
From Thy world, O Lord.
Mine is the right to decide
And I have chosen.
In the cold, amidst violence,
I have chosen, O Lord,
The meaning of Freedom.[1]

The Olim[2]

The following quotations by Russian Jews living in Israel are excerpts of their interviews given in Jerusalem, December 1984, for the film **Gates of Brass**. The complete text of these interviews is available by writing to us.

[1] *Dr. Semyon Gluzman. Composed Perm Labour Camp, Strict Regime, Siberia, USSR, 1979.*
[2] *Hebrew word for those that have immigrated to Israel.*

Esther Markish

Esther Markish is a vibrant woman of letters and the widow of the renowned Yiddish poet, Perets Markish.

'My husband, Perets Markish was one of the greatest Jewish poets who wrote in Yiddish and Russian . . .

. . . By 1948 the Israeli Embassy was opened in Moscow. For many Jews this was – on one hand – an extremely joyful event; but – on the other hand – it put us on guard. I shall give one example. Perets and I received an invitation to one of the Embassy's receptions. They told us about it over the phone from the Soviet Writer's Union and immediately added, "But we don't recommend that you go to this reception." . . .

. . . This basic group of which my husband was a part, was shot four years after their arrest on August 12, 1952, which is now known as the "Night of the Murdered Poets." They were part of the Jewish Anti-Fascist Committee.

Today with hindsight it is clear that this was an effort to cut off the head of the Jewish people, to deprive them of their spiritual leaders; and, having left this people without culture, to turn them simply into a herd of sheep. But it didn't succeed because Stalin died. He died in time for those who survived; but, unfortunately, it was half a year too late for those whose fate had been decided. And had Perets lived just another half year, he would have been saved from Stalin's paranoia. But it so happened that they were shot half a year before Stalin's death . . . . By 1953 pogroms had already started in Moscow out in the open and it was impossible for a Jew to walk unmolested in the street. They beat little children in the schools and screamed at them: "Vile murderers, zhids!" so that it was clear to everyone that the end had come for the Jews . . .

. . . They took us away and under the harshest conditions in railway cattle cars brought us to Kazakhstan where we were to supposed to live for 10 years . . .

. . . When my turn came, I went up to the office of General Boris Oglebsky. He rose and smiling came toward me and asked, "You guessed why you are here?"

I had guessed. I had guessed and I was terrified. But I wanted to hear from his lips everything that could be learned about my husband.

I answered him with half-dead lips, "No, I am here for you to inform me of the fate of my husband."

And then, moving a glass of water toward me, he said, "Your husband was shot on August 12th 1952." . . . '

David Markish

David Markish, who left the USSR in 1972, is a well-known Israeli author and the President of the Russian section of the Union of writers in Israel.

' . . . The first Israeli Embassy opened near our home in Moscow on Gorky Street with flags and all the other attributes. When I went to school – I was then 10 or 11 years old – I always made a detour and passed by the Embassy to look at the flag. I used to stand guard there because I wanted to see how a Jew with an Israeli passport looked; an independent Jew with his own land and his own government . . .

. . . Soviet Jewry was supposed to have been

exiled from the major cities and centres to Siberia and Kazkhstan and barracks were constructed along the Far East railroad line. Probably they are still standing to this day, if they haven't yet collapsed. This was supposed to be the end of the action against Soviet Jewry. This is a fact, not a fantasy; a fact based on data at our disposal.

As you know, it ended fortunately for Soviet Jewry and for all Jewry with the death of Stalin. He died when he was destined to die, of course; but if he had died a year later, I think that we would not be sitting here today and giving this interview . . .

. . . I think that there are three books which revived the interest of Soviet Jewry in their heritage: **The Judean War**, later **Exodus**, and always the **Bible** . . .

Dr. Lazar Liubarsky

Dr. Lazar Liubarsky, a 50-year-old engineer from Rostov-on-Don, was in refusal for seven years. He and his wife and two daughters left the USSR in 1977. We recorded part of his story as follows:

' . . . I, an engineer, worked in an engineering world far from the humanitarian Bohemia. Therefore, I loved culture – and especially Russian culture – very much. I didn't think about being a Jew because I was a card-carrying member of the Communist Party. But something happened to change this.

In 1957, when stopping at a book counter on the streets of Moscow, I saw a small volume with "Perets Markish" written on the cover. I opened the book and the words "a translation from the Yiddish" leapt out at me. Until that time I had never heard of this author's name. I leafed through quickly and my glance stopped at a poem entitled "The Inextinguishable Lamp". I was struck by the first lines of the poem where Perets Markish drew a parallel between the destruction of 6 million Jewish victims of the Holocaust and the killing of Soviet Jewish playwright, Mikhoels. The words at the end particularly spoke to me: " . . . Accessible, like the forest, like the foam of free waters, like the sun and with you in the dream about a better fate . . ."

. . . These words have returned to me over and over again. I sensed at that moment that I was already stepping out onto another path to dream of a better fate.

I must mention that during these four years of imprisonment my mother and father died. My father, at first calmly, began little-by-little to insert some Jewish words in his letters. Not one of those letters ever reached me. Not one letter from the West was ever given to me, although once every two months the administration of the camp spilled out a whole portfolio of letters in front of me and intimidated me: "You see, you are serving time; but your crime continues because your allies, the Zionists, imperialists of every stripe and colour, continue their connection with you, continue to encourage you. And since you did not acknowledge that you are not in alliance with them; otherwise, you will not get out of here."

It continued like that until the last day . . .'

Luba Bar Menachem

We interviewed Luba Bar Menachem in her apartment in the Jewish Quarter of the Old City of Jerusalem. She is a graphic artist and her husband is a physician. They have three children. She left the Soviet Union in April 1971.

' . . . Yiddish had not been spoken in our family for three generations. The Sabbath was not kept; and really, our parents never told us we were Jews.

Somehow it happened that I went to school and was just like all the other children; and the fact of my being Jewish became known to me at a very late date. It happened on a holiday when I accidentally saw my parents passport which had "Jew" or **evri** written under Section 5. It was a terrible shock to me, for **Jew** until then was a dirty word. When children were fighting and hitting each other the last word would always be, "You Jew!"

And suddenly it was me who was Jewish also. The first thing I did, I just cried and waited for my mother to come home. When she came home, I asked her, "It is really true that we are Jews?" And she said, "Yes, we are Jews – just like there are other nationalities, Ukranians, Russians – we are Jews. There's no reason to be angry or ashamed. On the contrary, it's a reason to be proud because Jews did a lot of good things for the world. They did a lot for Russia; and if you examine world history, you will see there are a lot of things Jews invented or gave or contributed."

That didn't make me feel any better. I still suffered from the fact that I was a Jew and I still hid the fact in every possible way. I didn't want the children in school to know, or my girl friends. For I was like all kids that want to be similar to everyone else . . .

. . . Sometimes we met to celebrate some Jewish holiday or just to talk about Israel, or to exchange news we had heard or to share letters we received from Israel. Those letters sometimes were postcards with two words written on them, or a New Year's card, and that would warm our hearts for many weeks . . .

. . . Father died in hospital without having a soul from his own family at his side – children or any relative – alone completely. On the telephone he begged us so many times, "I don't want to die in hospital with a nurse beside me; I want to die with you beside me."

And that little difference – he could have died in a hospital in Israel and we could have been beside him – is a cardinal difference. To deprive someone of a very basic right is not to allow them to die where they want to.'

Yuri, Tanya, and Lisa Kolker

Yuri, Tanya and Lisa Kolker left the Soviet Union in 1984. Their exit visas were 3 out of the 896 visas that were granted by the Soviet authorities during this year of the lowest Jewish emigration from the USSR in recent history. The interviews begin with Yuri speaking.

' . . . Our life was difficult. But there is a moment of truth. In the long run the lie becomes unbearable. When they lie and lie and lie day after day . . . There are people who simply are insensitive to lying. It becomes unbearable. The lie is everywhere: lies from above, lies from below, lies from all levels. For me this was the most important motive for leaving . . .

. . . From the scientific institute I went to a boiler room and worked there about four years. The nervous tension was very great; but the thing that worried us the most was that we simply were unable to make ends meet. The threat of hunger hung over us because when I went to work in the boiler room, I earned substantially less than I had in the scientific research institute. My wife was then a second degree invalid and was receiving a pension . . .

. . . In late 1982, early 1983, a new, violent wave of anti-Semitism began from above. There were endless newspaper articles every week that would appear in the Leningrad central newspapers – articles of ambiguous content but understood completely by millions of readers. In the Soviet Union it is impossible to declare a "Kristalnacht" as was done in Germany. It's not possible to call a nightmare by its proper name. They can't say: "We don't like Jews." They have to say it in other words.

In the late forties and early fifties, there was a campaign against "cosmopolitans". They thought up the word cosmopolitan but no-one doubted that the Jews were being discussed. Now it's different; now they speak about "Zionists"; but in fact they are talking about Jews and everyone understands this too. I want to say that a new campaign of slander has begun and I have the impression that the newspapers – that is the mass media – are preparing public opinion for some kind of changes. I won't attempt to predict what these will be. Just before Stalin's death there were preparations to exile all the Jews to Siberia beyond the Urals mountain range. Perhaps now too some kind of mass action is being prepared. I don't know. Apparently, if a pogrom will take place, it will be a quiet, specific pogrom. In the Soviet Union they understand that now the West will react to the direct spilling of blood. Therefore, they won't knife but will suffocate people . . .

. . . I now want to speak about my Christian Russian Orthodox friend, Martynov, who has taken the dangerous position of challenging Soviet anti-Semitism. Martynov is an absolutely unique person. I know him very well and I think that in recent years no-one did more than he to expose governmental anti-Semitism. What did he do?

It should be said that Martynov has a long established record as a human rights defender. It began very simply. He defended his unjustly offended co-workers and acquaintnaces. Gradually he acquired a reputation for this. I should add that Martynov is a world-renowned scholar, a bibliographer, archivist, and historian of literature. He studied Russian literature of the eighteenth century, then Russian poetry of the Silver Age, during the end of the nineteenth and beginning of the twentieth centuries. He has produced two monographs and over 150 publications . . .

. . . Around the end of 1982 and beginning of 1983, Martynov began systematically to investigate the works of a contemporary Soviet journalist, the anti-Semite Lev Korneev, a man devoid of conscience. Martynov wrote a tractate based on Soviet sources exposing the falsifications of Lev Korneev. It turned out to be a work of 50 to 60 typed pages which he offered to Soviet publishers and journals. He not only exposed anti-Semitism, but anti-Semites.

The important thing here is that according to Soviet laws, if Martynov would have said, “In the Soviet Union there is anti-Semitism,” he would immediately be put behind bars. But he said it differently: “In the Soviet Union there are anti-

Semites – for example, Lev Korneev." He proved his point by using concrete facts.

He did not succeed in publishing his work in Russia; but it attracted attention in the West, right up to the American Congress. There are letters – statements by members of both Houses – and it was Martynov who pointed this out. This was his service to the Jews and for this reason I think that we should support him . . .

. . . I wouldn't attempt to say how many Jews would leave if the borders were open. Probably all.'

Tanya Kolker

'. . . We became refuseniks when we received our first refusal in 1980. We got more information about Israel, and then I began to think that perhaps we would go to Israel and not simply leave the USSR. Moreover the woman who sent us the necessary official invitation from Israel turned out to be a very kind, sympathetic person. She sent us remarkable letters which changed my attitude here. I think that we were unusually lucky, that it was some kind of miracle, some good fortune that we left there because in the last years I lived in constant terror . . .

. . . Why they let us go instead of imprisoning us to teach others a lesson is still incomprehensible. I perceive this as a miracle and constantly rejoice at the good fortune that we left. I'm also happy for my daughter since for Liza the last years were very difficult, perhaps even more so than for us. The teacher was an anti-Semite. The child lived a dual life because at home she heard all our conversation. We had one room and that meant that our discussions took place in her presence.

She is already old enough to understand.

And in school it was entirely different. There was ideological propaganda there – totally monstrous ideological violence against children in the literal sense of the word. She was accepted into the "Pioneers"[1] and it was difficult for her because her parents had more influence. Naturally she believed in them more than in the school. It was perhaps more difficult for her than for us because we didn't have to lie . . .'

Liza Kolker – 11 years old

' . . . There were also Jewish girls in our school who were accused of being drug addicts, of taking drugs. We had a dining room where they fed us and they probably planted the drugs in the girl's possession. Then it was analysed as drugs and some of the girls were simply sent away from Leningrad together.'

Igor Tufeld

Igor Tufeld left the Soviet Union in 1977 at the age of 20. He had to leave his parents in Moscow who are sickly. He has worked tirelessly to have them released to no avail.

'I first learned that I was a Jew when I was a little boy only five years old and it happened very unexpectedly. I was playing with the neighbouring little children and suddenly I heard one boy, who was even younger than I – three or four years old – say to me, "zhid". I didn't understand at first what was going on, but I guessed that it was something bad. Later when I came home and asked my parents, they explained to me what a **zhid** was. They explained that we were all Jews and that this

[1] *Communist Youth Organization.*

was not a very pleasant designation for a Jew. I remember that I was very distressed by this and I even began to cry and said that I did not want to be a Jew. That first impression has remained for all these years and I am certain I shall never forget it . . .'

Yigal Gorodetsky

Yigal Gorodetsky is a 39-year-old writer, and editor of the **Israel Today** magazine.

'. . . It needs to be said that the actions of the KGB in the Soviet Union resemble that of some illegal organization. They try to present matters as if we Jews who want to leave for Israel are acting illegally; but, on the contrary, they the KGB are acting illegally. For example, when they summoned me there was no protocol on the table, nothing was written down. They tried to present it all as a conversation; they didn't even summon me with a note, but rather a man came and led me to their conspiratorial apartment. There was no sign on the door. There was only a secret lock. It was in the most ordinary home; outside everything was arranged as if it were the most ordinary apartment.

The KGB tried not to introduce themselves, not show their documents. Of course I demanded it; they would have been forced to show them. And when I tried to put everything on an official footing I came up against a stone wall. They didn't want to do that. They didn't want there to be any traces. I would never be able to prove anything – that I had contact with some kind of organization. They talked with me trying to draw something out of me, to grope for something. Apparently if they would find something then they could concoct some kind of case. But when they encountered resistance, active resistance, at least in those liberal days when I left, then they retreated. Retreated! It's possible to fight against this organization. The chief thing is not to be afraid, not to fear. It's necessary to put everything on an official footing. That's what **they** fear.'

Dr. Lev Utevsky

Dr. Lev Utevsky, 50 years of age, is a Professor of Applied Polymer Chemistry engaged today in research work at the University of Beersheva. He left Leningrad in 1980 and all of his family have since joined him in Israel.

' . . . Unfortunately, recent events show that this decision is developing in the direction of a return to the worst Stalinist times of the fifties. This is apparent primarily in the pogrom-like anti-Semitic propaganda in the Soviet press, propaganda which didn't exist even during Stalin's time.

Here is one such example. It is a copy of the journal **Zvezda vostoka**[1], published in the Moslem Republic of Uzbekistan in 1984, although in Russian. This article was written by Lev Korneev, a very well-known anti-Semite, who stands out even among Soviet official propagandists and who is very widely published.

In this article he says that anti-semitism is always against exploiters and against religious Jews, not Jews in general. He calls Judaism an ideology of money-grubbing racism and aspirations to world domination expressed in the form of religion. He says that hatred of religious Jews could grow into hatred of all Jews without exception and take the form of pogroms, beating of

[1] ***Star of the East***

children, women, and old people. The hatred of the masses, exploited by Jewish traders, merchants, usurers, tavern-keepers, and the like, could turn not only against these bloodsuckers, but also against their families and even against that segment of working Jews who didn't participate directly in exploitation.

What is that if not a call for a pogrom? That is the general situation today . . .

. . . What is qualitatively new is the system of threats and blackmail which was used before his arrest. A KGB colonel, in this case, Colonel Krasnov, directly threatened Levin that if he did not stop his religious activity he would be thrown in jail and his fiancee Yudit Nepomnyashchaya, also a Hebrew teacher, would be thrown into a room of criminals who would rape her in front of his eyes. Such bandit-type threats are new in KGB practice. More and more frequently KGB officers say directly: "We shall crush you; we shall destroy you . . ."

. . . You have to understand that the attack is conducted not against some separate forms of Jewish activity, but against all Jewish life. The same Colonel Krasnov said, "I shall abolish your Sabbaths and holidays."[1]

Tatyana Greengot and Sasha

Tatyana Greengot is 34 years old and and raising her seven-year-old son Sasha alone. She is by profession a computer programming engineer. Sasha's father, Michael Beizar is in refusal in Leningrad. He works as a guide for Jewish points of interest in Leningrad. Sasha has lost the sight of

[1] *Statements in personal letters to Dr. Lev Utevsky from his Jewish contacts in the Soviet Union.*

one eye due to a freak accident after their arrival in Israel.

Question: 'Do you still have hope that one day you'll be re-united?
Tatyana: 'Of course there is hope. Without hope, it's impossible to live. I hope that finally the situation will change and that he will come here to us . . .'

Dr. Edward Ussoskin
Dr. Edward Ussoskin, and electronic engineer, has championed the cause of the Jews in Russia since his departure with his wife and two sons in 1978. He came from the city of Leningrad where he left behind his two sisters. He stays in close touch with many of the refuseniks in Leningrad and he has become an important link to the Western media on their current status. He has thousands of names of refuseniks on his personal computer and sends out letters of encouragement and hope to them on a regular basis. His letters penetrate the Iron Curtain as they are written in Russian. His personal efforts for his own people are to be commended and he is helped to some degree financially by the Union of Councils of Soviet Jewry, particularly the Chicago group. He speaks out on behalf of his friends.

' . . . On the day of his arrival in the camp, Zakhar was beaten. They kicked his face with their boots, hit him on the kidneys and liver, beat him wherever they could. He was beaten by criminal prisoners, demanding that he be a model activist, a model Soviet prisoner. If not, they told him he would receive another term of three years. The following day, when Zakhar half-alive crawled out they forced him to go to work. The head of the convoy told him, "Hitler didn't destroy enough of you Jews." And he ordered the head of the guard, "If that one so much as stirs during work, shoot him right away."

Tatyana Zunshain arrived at her husband's labour camp psychologically broken. The KGB had persecuted her constantly. In Leningrad they summoned her for interrogations, arrested her, followed her out of Leningrad, and did not let her speak on the telephone with relatives and friends abroad. She arrived broken but left her husband with her spirits lifted. Zakhar told her, "We don't belong to ourselves; we belong to the Jewish people and it's not important what happens to me. I shall not give in."

Also, I want to tell you the story about Fradkova. On July 18th Nadeshda Fradkova, a refusenik since 1978, began an unlimited hunger strike until she would receive her visa to leave for the State of Israel. When they dragged her from her apartment to the police car the KGB agents screamed at her, "You Zhid bitch! We'll finish you off!"

Since then Nadezhda has been in a prison psychiatric hospital. She is completely healthy mentally. This was confirmed by two American doctors who examined her in May of this year. The Soviet authorities told her that she is crazy because she wants to go to the State of Israel.

Nadezhda is under treatment, according to the official decision received by Boris Elkin. She is in a department for the use of new "mind-changing" medicines and methods. These are Mengele-like methods of dealing with Jewish activists. Until now we have not known of such treatment of Jews who only want to leave for their own country, Israel . . .'

Emma Lifshitz

Emma Lifshitz is the beautiful, young wife of Alex Lifshitz, one of the most renowned Russian ballet teachers and choreographers. His students included Mikhael Baryshnikov, Rudolf Nureyev and Valery Panov. Together they have established an academy of ballet in Jerusalem.

' . . . Our departure was a somewhat sad story. Alex wrote several books. He published short sketches and poems in newspapers and journals, but it was impossible to take them out. He had a very good work on choreography which was supposed to be published. Well, naturally, we were unable to take it out. He had a colossal library of about 2,000 volumes of very rare books which he had collected all of his life and interesting musical recordings which we were also forced to leave behind. It was a tragedy to part with them . . . '

Valery Kukui

Valery Kukui left the Soviet Union in 1974. He is 46 years old, and works as an official in the city hall in Arad, a development town in the Negev Desert in Israel.

' . . . At one time the synagogue was closed because of alleged urban renewal in the part of the city where is was located. A promise was given orally that at some time the possibility of opening it in another spot would be investigated. To this day it has not been opened; and moreover, when the observant Jews assemble in order to pray on some religious holiday, the KGB intimidate them and they are forced to pray only in secret . . .

. . . A Soviet camp is a carbon copy of Soviet society. It is territory surrounded by a fence around which stand machine gunners with Kalashnikov rifles, who kill anyone who tries to leave either by jumping or crawling over the fence. The camp is a society which is full of corruption, full of inequality, full of all possible restrictions. It is a framework which destroys man, it corrects no-one, although it is called a "corrective labour camp." The camp did not crush me morally. I was prepared for it by my entire life. As long as I lived in that society I felt myself a prisoner of it. Physically it caused me damage, of course. I left the camp with several illnesses that I had acquired there; but my spirit grew stronger.'

Dr. Lev Roitburd

Dr. Lev Roitburd is a mechanical engineer who lives in Tel Aviv. He left Odessa in January 1981, and was in refusal with his wife and son for 9 years. He was put in prison in the USSR and has suffered a permanently disabling back injury as a result.

'I was born in 1936 in a small shtetl not far from Odessa which was practically a Jewish town before the war. During the war, in 1944 the entire Jewish population which had not managed to be evacuated – 940 people in all – were killed in one day. In front of mothers and fathers they shot children first, then women, and then they shot the men and older people. The shooting was done by Ukranian nationals under the direction of the Nazis. One of them was accidentally identified in 1960; and in 1961 they held a show trial in which individual pictures of this mass shooting were displayed. Strange as it seems, the Nazis and

Ukranian nationals who shot the Jews enjoyed their handiwork and therefore some photographs of this barbaric murder were preserved. By the way a large part of my relatives perished there . . .

. . . As a result of all of our experiences the Soviet authorities tried to categorize what they called our Zionist, chauvinist activity as truly anti-Soviet. I want to note that neither I nor my friends nor those who today are trying to leave the Soviet Union had any thoughts or desires of fighting against the Soviet regime. They wish only to leave the Soviet Union or to receive the opportunity to develop Jewish culture in the Soviet Union, to study their Hebrew language freely, and to profess their faith without pressure or punishment. In fact, everyone knows that today if the Jewish religion as such exists in the Soviet Union, it exists under continual duress as does the language. Today there are not only no Jewish cemetaries, but also no Christian or Catholic cemetaries. All are combined in non-sectarian common burial grounds . . .

. . . I want to say a few words about the Soviet system of re-education in camps. Naturally I and all our friends who are serving time now experience the most difficult conditions because they usually select for us the most distant and coldest camps. Warm clothing is not permitted – woolen underwear, sweaters, scarves, gloves and padded jackets are forbidden.

A day's food ration is budgeted at 37 kopeks[1] per prisoner. As a result of such a 'fortified' diet, during the first three to four months, I lost over 20 kilos. Naturally, after this it is no longer possible to lose more weight since only bones are left.

The system is constructed to bring a man to the

[1] *Approximate equivalent of $0.25 US.*

point of exhaustion, to suppress him psychologically and morally. If that doesn't succeed, they try to incite the criminals against him.

... The living conditions are 70 men in a barracks with a bath at best once a week, with practically no hot water. We had a cinema which in winter is called "Snowdrop" and in summer "Raindrop" because it is out on the street. They show only patriotic Soviet films and there is practically nothing to see. In the library you can't take out a book which you want – all this plus separation from one's family is discouraging.

In addition to the years you're serving time, your health is destroyed for many years after your release. People return from the camps sick. I was released from the camp with such stomach problems that I had to follow a very strict diet for a year. My gums were bleeding and bleed to this day. I had a problem with my spine because the work which I did was very hard. First I dragged wood and boards along the road to camp; and, later in the camp zone, I mixed cement. In the zone it was called the "Road of Death" because you had to wade through a knee-deep swamp and drag a heavy load weighing several hundred kilos on a two-wheeled cart. This exhausts a poorly fed man to the ultimate degree. Thus my term passed ...'

Ruth Alexandrovich

Ruth Alexandrovich now resides in Jerusalem and nurses in an "old age" home.

She has one son and no longer has any family members in Russia.

'... The situation was really very serious. At the

same time the situation outside the prison was also very grave, for they had also arrested groups of youths in Kishinev and Leningrad. We all sat in prison facing the same charges awaiting trial.

At that time my mother succeeded in obtaining a visa for Israel, a month before my trial. She took my brother, who otherwise would have been drafted by the Soviet army, and they left for Israel. Mama was in Israel for one day and immediately left for the States where she stirred up public opinion and started a campaign to help all of us who had been arrested. This helped a lot, and instead of the expected seven years, I received one year. The group of three fellows with me received half of what they could haved received. I believe this reduction came because of the response which Mama found in Europe, but primarily in America. People in the very highest positions became involved and helped. I think that today these things can and should be repeated . . .

The work was supposedly light. We had to sew sleeves made of tarpaulin[1]. Soon there wasn't any skin left on my hands because of the roughness of the canvas. We had a quota which it was impossible to fulfill in eight hours. It was therefore necessary to sit and sew for 12 or 13 hours. If the quota was not fulfilled, then there were all kinds of punishments. For example the cancellation of letters or packages or visitors from home.

During the whole time I had one meeting with my father. He was supposed to receive a meeting with me for three days, as the law permits; but for some reason they gave him only a day and a half. People were able to write me many letters, but I could write very few in return. I must note that those

[1] *Heavy canvas*

letters which I received both from Riga and from Moscow and some from abroad which came via my father were a great help to me . . .

. . . Now, in recent years things are entirely different. Now they attempt to try a political prisoner according to a criminal statute and then he lands in a criminal camp. The criminal crowd are murderers, rapists, and thieves from the underground world, and it is next to impossible to associate with them, male or female. We all know this to be true from friends who now are in these camps. The food there is worse and the regulations about letters and packages are much stricter. Everything is much worse; but the main thing is that no spiritual or cultural life exists there.

In my camp I was able somehow to exchange information with a Ukranian woman who had then served 20 years of her 25-year sentence. She told me about their history and her life which was interesting and useful spiritual nourishment. A person who lands in such a camp today has no way out because there is no one to talk to or to associate with. In addition today the authorities frequently incite this criminal society to anti-semitic attacks or to 'anti'-anything which is helpful to them. The people who land in camps today suffer very, very much.'

Jewish Emigration From The USSR Statistics[1]

1967	4,498	1974	20,628	1979	51,320
1970	4,235	1975	13,221	1980	21,471
1971	13,022	1976	14,261	1981	9,447
1972	31,681	1977	16,736	1982	2,688
1973	34,733	1978	28,864	1983	1,314
				1984	896

[1] National Conference on Soviet Jewry Research Bureau, January 1985. Publication, Washington Office, 2027 Massachusetts Avenue, N.W., Washington D.C. 20036, U.S.A.

From October 1968 to December 1984, 264,517 persons left the Soviet Union with Israeli visas. Approximately 163,209 of them went to Israel.

Discrimination Against Judaism

There are today fewer than sixty synagogues in the USSR and only five ordained rabbis. Unlike other religious groups in the USSR Jews are denied, among other things, the opportunity to train clergy, to form all-Soviet or regional organisations, or to publish religious bulletins or periodicals. No Hebrew Bible has been published in the USSR for over half a century and Jewish religious appurtenances such as prayer, shawls, mezuzot, and phylacteries are virtually unobtainable.

"The Prisoners of Zion"

Over 25 are serving terms of imprisonment or exile on trumped-up charges. Their real "crime" was their active struggle to secure their right to emigrate to Israel, or the right of Jews to live as Jews free from discrimination in the USSR.

The "Prisoners of Zion" are: Moshe Abramov; Yosef Begun, who has already served two terms of Siberian exile and has now been sentenced to seven years in prison and five years in exile; Yosef Berenshtein; Yuli Edelshtein; Nadezhda Fradkova; Boris Kanevsky; Aleksander Kholmiansky; Feliks Kochubievsky; Ya'acov Levin; Mark Nepomnyashchy; Dan Shapira; Anatoly Shcharansky; Lev Shefer; Simon Shnirman, who has already served a term of imprisonment and is now serving his second term; Yury Tarnopolsky; Alexander Yakir; Stanislav Zubko; and Zakhar Zunshain.

A non-Jew, Yuri Fiodorov, remains imprisoned

for helping his Jewish friends in the Leningrad airplane episode of 1970.

Twenty-one former "Prisoners of Zion" having served their terms of punishment in full, are still not being allowed to leave the USSR. These are: Victor Brailovsky, Boris Chernobilaky; Lev Elbert; Kim Fridman; Grigory Goishis; Grigory Goldshtein; Boris Kalendarev; Valadmir Klislik; Evgeny Lein; Osip Lokshin; Mark Naspitz; Ida Nudel; Mark Ochertiansky; Alexander Panariev; Alexander Paritsky; Dimitri Shchiglik; Isaak Shkolnik: Victor Shtilbans; Vladmir Slepak; Vladmir Tsurkerman; and Alexander Vilig.

The Law

The Soviet Union has ratified nearly all the major International Conventions dealing with human rights and has associated itself with the principal declarations dealing with human rights. In addition, the USSR Constitution and legislation purportedly contain guarantees of basic human rights.

The factual situation summarised above represents a massive violation by the Soviet authorities of the individual and collective rights of Soviet Jews as set forth both in these international human rights conventions and declarations, and in the Soviet Constitution and legislation.

Limitations of space permit only a very partial listing of the relevant provisions.

The principle of freedom of emigration has been incorporated in so many declarations and conventions that it may properly be regarded as a part of customary International Law. In addition, the Soviet Union is a party to the International

Covenant of Civil and Political Rights, Article 212 of which stipulates that "everyone has the right to leave any country, including his own" as well as the International Convention on the elimination of all forms of racial discrimination which gives expression to the same principle in Article 5:d. The Helsinki Final Act in Principle VII of Basket One incorporates a commitment by the signatories to act in conformity with the Universal Declaration of Human Rights by which they may be bound. The provisions on freedom of emigration contained in these instruments are reinforced by Basket Three of the Final Act which requires that especially favourable consideration be given to cases of family reunification.

The dismissal of applicants for exit visas from their jobs is a clear violation of Convention No.111 of the International Labour Organisation (ILO) concerning Discrimination in Respect of Employment and Occupation while their prosecution as "parasites" violates Convention No.29 of the ILO Concerning Forced or Compulsory Labour.

So far as the suppression of Jewish culture and Hebrew language is concerned, the Soviet government is obligated to respect the right of the Jewish minority "to enjoy their own culture, to profess and practise their own religion, or to use their own language" as expressed in Article 27 of the International Covenant on Civil and Political Rights and to enable the Jewish minority " . . . to carry on its own educational activities . . . including the use or the teaching of their own language." In addition, the discriminatory suppression of Hebrew violates the USSR Constitution itself,

Articles 34, 36, and 45, and Soviet law. For example the Russian Republic Criminal Code, Article 74, prohibits any form of discrimination limitation regarding the national languages of the peoples of the USSR.

The discriminatory disabilities imposed on Judaism in the USSR violate not only Article 27 of the International Covenant on Civil and Political Rights as cited above, but also Article 18 of that same Covenant which requires that "everyone shall have the right to manifest his religion or belief in worship, observance, practice and teaching". They also contradict the Soviet government's pledges implied in its acceptance of the United Nations Declaration on the Elimination of All Forms of Intolerance and of Discrimination based on Religion or Belief. They are in conflict also with Article 52 of the USSR Constitution guaranteeing freedom of conscience.

The anti-semitic incitement and discrimination described violates not only the above mentioned anti-discrimination provisions of the International Covenant on Civil and Political Rights, USSR Constitution and criminal codes, but also Article 20 of the International Covenant on Civil and Political Rights which prohibits "any advocacy of national, racial or religious hatred that constitutes incitement to discrimination, hostility or violence."

The prosecution and incarceration of Prisoners of Zion have invariably been associated with violations of so many provisions of International covenants to which the USSR is a party that it is impossible for want of space to cite them all. The safeguards these provisions set forth are in nearly all cases embodied in the USSR Constitution and

Criminal Procedure Codes as well. The proceedings against these Jewish defendants have in every case involved all or nearly all of the following violations of rights: unjustifiable and prolonged pre-trial detention; gross misapplication of the substantive criminal law; denial of the right to a defence; denial of the right to call witnesses and present evidence at trial; violation of the obligation of the prosecution and judiciary to conduct a thorough, complete and objective analysis of the circumstances of the case; and the imposition of excessive and disproportionate punishment.

Anti-Semitism, Alive And Well Today

Where is Josef Begun? He was listed as "disappeared" from the Soviet labour camp where he is serving a 12-year sentence. Yosef has been a victim of Soviet cruelty and persecution since 1971 for the crime of wanting to emigrate to Israel.

'Begun has been transferred to Chestopol Prison in the Ural Mountains, the harshest prison in the Soviet Union,' Begun's family told friends in Israel in a recent telephone conversation. Begun suffers from a heart ailment."[1]

Write to: Inna Begun, USSR, Moscow, Raketny Boulevard, 11/2, Apartment 64.

Medieval Penal Conditions Imposed On Alexander Kholmiansky, Hebrew Teacher From Moscow

Michael Kholmiansky reported in a telephone conversation that his brother has been confined to a 1½ by 1½ meter cell for almost two months. Letters of support should be sent to : USSR,

[1] *Soviet Jewry Education and Information Center Update, January and February, 1985, 9 Albali Street, Jerusalem, Israel.*

Moscow, Kirovogradskaiay 24/1, Apartment 191, Kholmiansky, Michael.

Yuli Edelshtein Sentenced To Three Years

Moscow Aliya activist Yuli Edelshtein was sentenced on December 19th to three years of labour camp for possession of drugs which were planted in his apartment by the K.G.B. Please write to Yuli's wife: U.S.S.R, Moscow, Liningradski pr. 33/6, Apartment 601, Edelshtein, Tatiana.

Yosef Berenshtein Brutally Assaulted In Prison By Soviet Thugs . . . May Be Blinded For Life

Berenshtein, one of only a few Hebrew teachers in Kiev, was arrested on trumped-up charges of speculating in the sale of gravestones. He had travelled to Novograd-Volynsk to assist his sister in obtaining a Jewish burial stone for a relative who had died. Arrested for "physically assaulting a policeman" he was condemned on the tenth of December 1984 to four years of imprisonment. On the night of December 12th he was attacked by prisoners who slashed his face with broken glass; both eyes were mutilated. No medical attention was given him for a week. His family was told that "He had inflicted the bruises on himself by using a knife." One eye was removed from his head.[1] He has lost 99.4 per cent of his sight in the other eye. Home address: U.S.S.R., Kiev 252147, Entuziastov 35/140, Berenshtein, Fanya.

Michael Elman Harassed In Leningrad

Michael Elman, a religious refusenik, was interrogated and beaten twice since November 1984. During the first interrogation in November,

[1] ***Jerusalem Post.*** *30 April 1985, p. 3.*

Michael's pregnant wife Dina who was also present went into labour and had to be rushed to the hospital. The KGB told Michael to end all religious activity in Leningrad.

A healthy boy, David Tzvi, was born to the Elmans. During the circumcision which took place in a private apartment, the police attempted to force their way into the apartment to stop the ceremony.

The Elmans address: U.S.S.R., Leningrad 195267, Suzdalsky Prospekt 103-55, Elman, Michael and Dina.

9

The Response

What You Can Do To Help Soviet Jews!

'Remember those in prison as if you were their fellow prisoners, and those who are mistreated as if you yourselves were suffering.'

Hebrews 13:3 NIV

It is extremely important for you to understand that **you can make a difference** in alleviating the suffering of Jews in the Soviet Union. But, it requires action. The following are suggested ways in which you can become involved. Let's not give any grounds for further poems like this:

A REFUSENIK'S CONCLUSIONS . . .

Don't be afraid of your foe,
The worst he can do is to kill you.
Don't be afraid of your friend,
The worst he can do is betray you.
Be afraid of those lulled by indifference.
It's because of their silent consent
That murder and betrayals are possible
By powers their uninvolvement lent.

Anonymous.

Also we must always remember that persecution in the Soviet Union is not restricted to the Jews, but also includes other religeous groups such as fundamental Christian believers. The **Voice Of Martyrs** magazine, March 1983 stated, 'In twelve years, the Soviet Communists arrested 25,000 Baptist pastors; 22,000 died in concentration camps and 1,000 Christians are known to be in jail now in the USSR alone. Who knows how many have disappeared into the Gulag?'

Media Pressure

The Soviet Jews need to know what kind of friends they have in us. Are we the kind of people they can depend on to conteract the hate literature and lying media presentations that surround them? A few films and TV programs have been made in the West on the issue of Soviet Jewry, but nothing has had a world-wide impact to mobilize a large base of support on their behalf. This was one reason why we began our "Gates of Brass" film project.

It has been proved that people in North America on the average spend three to five hours a year reading and more than two thousand hours yearly watching television. We in the West have become TV junkies. Therefore we are compelled to televise the important aspects of their lives in the USSR. We have designed "GATES OF BRASS" as a one-hour television program and at fifty-four minutes it is also usable in a special evening film presentation in a public forum. I suggest this format since a film showing in a closed theatre or auditorium will have an enormous effect on the viewing audience. The film is designed to make people want to get involved with helping the Soviet Jews. When the people come out of the theatre, they must have the opportunity to do several things:

1. Write to a refusenik to offer friendship and moral support.
2. Sign a petition demanding local government action on behalf of Soviet Jews and their rights.
3. Send protest letters in Russian to the Soviet Union leadership in the Kremlin.
4. Telephone their local government representative and suggest they bring the issue of Soviet Jewry up to the next level, until it reaches the head of your country.

"Gates Of Brass"

In order to obtain "Gates Of Brass" in book or video format, for information please contact **International Vistas** offices in Canada, Great Britain, Israel, South Africa and the USA. See the order form at the back of the book.

As you start to show the film or video cassette in your area you become a **mobilized** supporter of freedom for Soviet Jewry. By your actions you have proved your love and friendship. These very courageous men and women inside the Soviet Union deserve our very best efforts.

Lifeline Letters

If you like, you may adopt a Russian Jewish

family and open up a lifelong friendship through the mail until they are released. We will help you with updates and factual information from Israel. The Soviet Jews need to know more about their homeland.

Individuals, families, or groups can adopt a Refusenik family. If you are writing as a member of a Jewish or Christian group, do not say that you are writing as a member. You are writing as a concerned individual (otherwise, your letter may be confiscated as "Christian or Zionist" agitation.)

The "adoption" may consist only of written correspondence between you and your adopted family, or it may be expanded to include seeking the help of legislators, congressmen and senators, on behalf of the Refuseniks.

Refuseniks will not get in trouble if we write

Only those Refuseniks who have indicated that they wish to receive letters are included in the program. Adoptees often have said that such communication is "life insurance".

Make your letters warm and friendly. Write as you would to a member of your own family. Tell about your family, job, studies, travels and hobbies. Include a picture of you or your family, if you wish and ask for a picture of their family in return. Early in your correspondence attempt to establish the birthdates of all members of the family. Birthdays are very important celebrations in Russian culture, and they are excellent times to remember to send a special card in the mail.

When sending your letter, please purchase from the Post Office a registered, return receipt, requested by Air Mail. Keep the Receipt. For a minimal cost this ensures the delivery of your letter.

What To Avoid In Your Letter

– Avoid mentioning names of religious organisations.

– Avoid political criticism of Russia or the government of satellite countries i.e. the Communist countries.

– Avoid mentioning Israel in your first letters until you are sure your letters have gone through. Refer to "homeland", "land where it is warm", "place where we hope to meet someday", etc . . .

– Avoid anything provocative or accusatory about the USSR or any satellite countries' government. Do not indicate in any way that you wish the person were free or that you are seeking his or her release. **Don't** include any political or anti-Soviet statements.

Political Pressure

Here is where YOU come in. You have power in your society. You must know and believe this. Your elected representatives should be listening to you and your demands as a constituent. If enough of you begin to pressure your Senator, Congressmen or Members of Parliament in your various areas, then if they are good representatives they will listen to your letters, calls, telegrams and personal visits and will place the issue of Soviet Jewry high on their list of priorities. This in turn will influence the leadership of your respective countries. A good example has been the personal involvement of the last two American presidents, Carter and Reagan in the whole matter of Soviet Jewry. Obviously they are listening to their people.

Telegrams And Phone Calls

Individuals sending thousands of telegrams can make the difference by pressuring their national governments of these issues. When Anotoly Shchransky was being harrassed in his jail cell, a large protest went up from the West. My telegram was sent to the Prime Minister of Canada and several days later the report came out that the Canadian Government was lodging official protests on his behalf. The Soviets must pay attention to this kind of protest because of their desperate need for Canadian wheat.

Phone calls are also a quick way to get your petitions and protests across to government leaders. Letters, of course, are also very important. In addition to your local and national leaders, include special messages to communist parties in the free world. Send your appeals to:

U.S.S.R.
RSFSR Moscow
The Kremlin
Mr. Gorbachev

President Ronald Reagan
The White House
Washington, DC,
U.S.A.

U.S.S.R.
RSFSR Moscow
Novosibirsk
KGB Chief
Mr. Viktor Chebrikov

U.S.S.R.
RSFSR Moscow
Ogareva No. 6,
Ministry of Internal Affairs
Mr. Vitaly Fedorchuk

Ambassador Anatoly Dobrynin
Embassy of the U.S.S.R.
1125 16th Street NW
Washington DC 20036, U.S.A.

U.S.S.R.
RSFSR Moscow
Ogareva No. 6
OVIR Chief Constantin Zotov

Ambassador Oleg Troyanovsky
Soviet Mission to the U.N.
36 East 67th Street,
New York, New York 10021,
U.S.A.

Mr. Javier Perez de Cuellar
Secretary General
The United Nations,
United Nations Plaza
New York, New York 10017, U.S.A.

U.S.S.R.
RSFSR Moscow
Dzerzhinskogo No. 2
Chairman of the State
Security Committee

Insist on the Soviet Union's adherance to the 1975 Helsinki Accord on the "universal Declaration of Human Rights" that it signed along with thirty-four other nations. The Agreement declares that every citizen has the right to leave any country, including his own, and to return to that country. Citizens also have the basic right to be reunited with their families living in other countries, and citizens have the right to pursue their own cultural identity and practice of religion. Soviet emigration policy, therefore, is **not** an "internal affair", as the Kremlin claims. Furthermore the Soviets have been violating the Agreement's guarantee of freedom of contact by intercepting mail, especially the invitations sent to Soviet Jews from their relatives in Israel, an indispensable document for requesting an exit visa.

Insist on linkage of trade, technology and cultural agreements made by your national leaders with the release of Sovet Jewry. Insist that the Kremlin be forced to meet its Helsinki commitments and end the harassment and persecution of Soviet Jewry. Such leverage can be very effective, but it will only be brought to bear on the USSR today through sustained public pressure. Wherever possible, **"flex your voting muscle."**

Demonstrations

Be creative in your approach. You can make an impact on local Soviet Embassies, Consulates, Trade Delegations, Aeroflot Airlines offices, Soviet artistic and cultural performances and sporting events, the world over.

The Soviets spend millions of dollars each year in displaying their human propaganda in the world. Soviet ballet, musicians, folk dance troupes, circus entertainers and athletes continually visit throughout the earth. Every time they appear, there should be mass demonstrations against their country's policies and even boycotts of their performances. This would certainly cause them to take notice of world-wide attitudes regarding their internal policies.

It is possible to organise a telephone campaign to jam the lines of such offices with protests of their treatment of Soviet Jews. No opportunity should be missed to stand up for truth and righteouness.

Protest Marches

We have participated in several protest marches that have drawn attention to the plight of the Soviet Jews in the eyes of politicians, the media, the average citizens and the Soviets in the various areas. Candlelit marches of placard-carrying Jews and Christians, some dressed in prison garb has been effective. Recently, a march which got a lot of attention was organised in Tel Aviv when women activists chained together and dressed in prison uniforms marched from embassy to embassy. These marches can also be augmented with student sit-ins. This will be guaranteed to draw attention to the issue of Soviet Jewry.

We must beware, however, as the Soviets are masters at the game of international diplomacy; they will make overt gestures that sound good but really reflect no change in policy. They will even sign international agreements without changing their internal policies. As long as no-one complains, they will continue and go to even greater extremes.

Example: Emigration was stopped and no world reaction.

Example: Jews were imprisoned on trumped-up charges; no reaction from the free world.

Example: Beatings of Jews in broad daylight and again no significant response.

This enables the Soviets to bully their own citizens while at the same time they sit smugly at the conference tables of the world. This must not continue.

Local Radio And TV

You must see yourself as someone who had valid opinions and potentially interesting information for your local news media. You should gather all the up-to-date information you can on the situation in the Soviet Union. This information may be obtained through the various organisations mentioned in Chapter Six. Then you should find out who the person is in charge of news gathering for your local radio and TV stations. You can then contact them by a respectful letter or telephone call and make a personal appointment. You must see them as people who are doing a job and that you can help them by giving them up-to-date, factual information. Generally they will respond to you positively. We have been on such news and talk shows, both on radio and TV about such issues. You must see these people in the media as your friends.

You can also make similar contacts with the print media, locally or nationally. Here I refer to newspapers, magazines and journals.

Shortwave Radio

One of the most powerful ways of encouraging the Jews in the Soviet Union is via short-wave radio. The Voice of America, Kol Israel, The British Broadcasting Corporation, The Canadian Broadcasting Corporation, Dutch Short Wave, Australian Broadcasting, Radio Free Europe, Trans World Radio, Far East Broadcasting, Voice of Hope Short Wave and many other radio stations continually beam into Russia.

The Soviet authorities try to jam or technically block these broadcasts but cannot stop them all. This is one way in which the Jews inside Russia can make contact with the West. Kol Israel is now broadcasting daily programs in Russian from Jerusalem and over 100,000 Soviet Jews listen regularly. Write to Kol Israel to encourage them to continue and even enlarge their coverage in the USSR, perhaps you could even support this station financially from time to time.

Kol Israel Russian Broadcasts,
Sara Manobla,
P.O. Box 1082,
91010 Jerusalem, Israel.

Inter-Religious Action

Find out personally what is being done on behalf of Soviet Jews locally, both in the Jewish Action Groups and committees and get on their mailing lists to find out their schedule of events and then **participate**. Meridel and I are active members of the Soviet Jewry Information Centre in Jerusalem and we try to attend all their functions. Be a friend and assist those who are already working for Soviet Jewry.

Contact the local Ministerial Association or fellowships. Give them information on the conditions in the Soviet Union and how they can help as well.

Contact local schools, both state and private who can in turn mobilise their students to write to and pray for Soviet Jewish children.

Contact local Sunday schools to challenge them to teach about the problems of Soviet Jews and Christians and challenge them to take some concrete action.

Personal Contacts

Find Christians who are already supporting Christians in the Soviet Union. These Soviet Christians should be encouraged to reach out to their local Jews.

Form a special church committee to organise action for Soviet Jewry and stir other Christians to get involved. Invite knowledgeable Jews to address your group.

Resources

List of Political Prisoners in the USSR – 1982 Edition.

USSR News Brief (bi-monthly newsletter on human rights). Both available from: Cahiers du Samizdat, 48 rue du Lac, 1050-Bruxelles, Belgium.

Union of Councils for Soviet Jews (association disseminating information), 1411 K Street NW, Suite 402, Washington DC 20005, USA.

The First Guidebook to Prisons and Concentration Camps of the Soviet Union, by Avraham Shifrin, June 1982, Bantam Books Inc, 666 Fifth Avenue, New York, New York, USA.

"Prisonland USSR" (1980 film, 30 minutes, colour, English narration: Documentary made by candid cameras in USSR). Research Centre – Psychoprisons and Forced Labour Concentration Camps of the USSR, PO Box 32, Zikhron Yaakov, Israel. (Attention: Avraham Shifrin, Executive Director.)

"The Right To Believe" (1979 film, English narration). Keston College Support Group, 9 Dalziel Place, Edinburgh EH7 5TR, Scotland.

"Gates of Brass" (1985 film, English narration). Jerusalem Vistas, PO Box 8232, Jerusalem, Israel. (Attention: Jay Rawlings.)

Personal Visits

You can even visit refuseniks in the USSR. If you are planning a trip to the USSR use it as an opportunity to visit some Jewish people. Please find out from your local Soviet Jewry council or committee, names and addresses in the cities where you are going and who wants to receive visitors. Ask what articles you could carry in that would be beneficial, such as medicine, food, books or clothing.

If you have read this book through you will find that you can no longer remain indifferent or inactive to the matter of freedom for Soviet Jewry. I believe that you will want to take action of some kind.

Prayer

All over the world people are praying round-the-clock for the release of Soviet Jews "en masse".

The following outline gives suggestions on how to pray for the Jews of Russia.

Study and learn the promises of God that speak about their release from Russia. Believers should then hold fast to these promises in prayer.

Read

Isaiah 43:5,6
Jeremiah 31:7,8-14
Isaiah 49:24-26
Jeremiah 3:12,18
Isaiah 11:11,12
Isaiah 14:1,32
Psalm 35:17
Jeremiah 16:14,15
Ezekiel 37:1-14
Psalm 102:19,20

Pray for **Hope** to be conveyed to the Jewish activists in their desperate situation. If they begin to know and understand that there are many people in the world who know their plight and care about them it will help to sustain them until they are released.

Read

Psalm 33:18-22
Ezekiel 37:11b,12
Jeremiah 31:16b,17

Pray That God would hear the crying and groaning of the Jews in Soviet Russia and remember His covenant with Abraham, Isaac and Jacob.

Read

Psalm 79:11
Exodus 2:23b-25

Pray that the persecution does not reach the point of no return with neo-Stalinists poised to effect the "final solution".

Pray for the Lord to raise up people who will continue to go into Russia to keep the contacts fresh with the rest of the world.

Pray also that the people who do go in will be properly prepared and will not put the Jews inside under further duress and pressure.

Pray that the Lord will put into the hearts of the Jews who do leave Russia to go to Israel.

Pray for the names of individual Jews being persecuted, their families and specific situations and needs.

Pray to know what part YOU can play in this movement outside of Russia to help those who are inside on the "front lines" of the battle.

Pray for the Spirit of God to give you discernment and understanding of Satan's devices and tactics. The arch-enemy of God is using the Soviet system as his agent to bring material and psychological deprivations against the Jews such as: threats, intimidations, harrassments, false accusations, beatings, tortures, imprisonment, lying, anti-semitic, anti-Zionist propaganda, false media programs, including film, newspaper articles and books. This attack is no longer just aimed at those Jews who desire to go to Israel; but every Jew, wherever he is in the USSR is "marked" simply because he is a Jew.

Pray to become an "intercessor" on behalf of Soviet Jews so that you stand on their behalf and are able to do battle in the Spirit realm for them. Rees Howells, in the book "Intercessor" mentions the twenty-four hour prayer watches kept at the

Bible College of Wales during World War Two. He and many others entered by the spirit into Nazi concentration camps, including the gas chambers, as they prayed for the Jewish people.

Read
Daniel 9
James 5:16b
Isaiah 59:16

Fast and Pray for the release of the prisoners.
Read
Isaiah 58:6,7
Esther 4:12-16

'Is not this the fast that I have chosen, to loose the bands of wickedness, to undo the heavy burdens, and to let the oppressed go free, and that ye break every yoke?'

Isaiah 58:6

'For if thou altogether holdest thy peace at this time, then shall there enlargement and deliverance arise to the Jews from another place; but thou and thy father's house shall be destroyed: and who knoweth whither thou art come to the kingdom for such a time as this?

Then Esther bade them return Mordecai this answer,

"Go, gather all the Jews that are present in Shushan, and fast ye for me, and neither eat nor drink three days, night or day: I also and my maidens will fast likewise; and so will I go in unto the king, which is not according to the law: and if I perish I perish." '

Esther 4:14-16

Pray for those Russians who persecute the Jews and Christians alike.

Read	Psalm 71:13
Psalm 35:6	Jeremiah 17:18
Psalm 83:12-18	Romans 12:14
Jeremiah 20:11	Matthew 5:44

Everyone has their part to play. I believe we can look with faith to divine intervention.

'Then they shall know that I am the Lord their God, which caused them to be led into captivity among the heathen: but I have gathered them unto their own land, and have LEFT NONE of them anymore there.

Neither will I hide my face anymore from them: for I have poured out my spirit upon the house of Israel, saith the Lord God.'

Ezekiel 39:28,29

JEWISH ORGANISATIONS HELPING SOVIET JEWS

Union of Councils For Soviet Jews,
Suite 402,
1411 K Street NW
Washington DC, USA, 2005.

The Union of Councils for Soviet Jews is a Washington-based independent organisation composed of thirty-seven local councils, three domestic affiliates, three international affiliates and fifty-five thousand individual members, dedicated to the freedom of immigration and human rights for all Soviet Jews. (Author's note – they publish an excellent newsletter.)

National Chairperson, Lynn Singer

35's The Women's Campaign for Soviet Jewry,
755A Finchley Road,
London NW11,
England.
Co-Chairman: Rita Eker, Margaret Rigal.

They provide excellent update material on current situations faced by Soviet Jews who are being harrassed and persecuted.

Research Centre for Prisons, Psychoprisons and Forced Labour Concentration Camps of the USSR.
Avraham Shifrin, Founder.
PO Box 132,
Zikron Yaacov, Israel.

Jews in the USSR – Weekly,
Nan Greifer, Editor,
31 Percy Street,
London W1P 9FG
England.
Very informative weekly.

Soviet Jewry Education and Information Centre,
9 Alkalai Street, Room 23,
Jerusalem 92223, Israel.
Dr. Yuri Stern, Director

A recently founded organisation to co-ordinate public action on behalf of Soviet Jewry in Israel. Administered by former Soviet refuseniks and activists. This is a very key organisation in the entire activist movement run by former Soviet Jews for Soviet Jewry in Israel.

The Israel Public Council for Soviet Jewry,
4a Chissin Street,
Tel Aviv, Israel.
Dr. Abe Harman, Chairman

Foreign Ministry of Israel Russian Department,
Professor Lapidot,
PO Box 7027,
Albert Mindler Street, 25,
Kiria, Tel Aviv, Israel.

Shamir: Association of Jewish Professionals from the Soviet Union and Eastern Europe in Israel.
6 David Yellin Street,
Jerusalem, Israel.
(02) 223-702
Founder and Director – Professor Herman Branover
Executive Director – Ilana Cover.

Scientists' Committee of the Israel Public Council for Soviet Jewry,
4a Chissin Street,
Tel Aviv 64284 Israel.
(03) 299-832 or 299-942.

National Conference on Soviet Jewry
10 East 40th Street, Suite 907,
New York, New York 10016, USA
(212) 679-6122
Executive Director – Jerry Goodman.

Student Struggle for Soviet Jewry,
210 West 91st Street,
New York, New York 10002, USA,
(212) 799-8900
National Co-ordinator – Glenn Richter.

International League for the Repatriation of Russian Jews,
315 Church Street, Suite 200,
New York, New York 10013, USA.
(212) 431-6866
President – Morris Brofman

Institute of Jewish Affairs,
11 Hertford Street,
London WIY 7DX, England.
Publishes "Soviet Jewish Affairs"
Director – Dr. J. Hirszovic.

New York Legal Coalition for Soviet Jewry,
New York Medical Committee on Soviet Jewry,
8 West 40th Street, Room 602,
New York, New York 10018, USA
(212) 354-1316

Medical Mobilisation for Soviet Jewry,
91 N. Franklin Street,
Hempstead, New York 11550, USA
(516) 538-5454

The Greater New York Conference on Soviet Jewry,
New York Women's Coalition for Soviet Jewry,
New York Legal Coalition for Soviet Jewry,
New York Mental Health Committee on Soviet Jewry,
8 West 40th Street,
New York, New York 10018, USA

National Lawyers Committee For Soviet Jewry,
National Business Advisory Council on Soviet Jewry,
10 East 40th Street,
New York, New York 10016, USA

Committee of Concerned Scientists,
9 East 40th Street,
New York, New York 10016, USA

CHRISTIAN ORGANISATIONS HELPING SOVIET JEWS

The International Christian Embassy, Jerusalem,
PO Box 1192,
Jerusalem, Israel.
Lilly Myss-Hansen – Produces a quarterly on Soviet Jews and regularly updated portfolios. Letter-writing to Western government leaders and Soviet officials, rallies throughout the world under the banner, "Mordecai Outcry"

are encouraged. Christians have collected thousands of signatures on petitions and sent them to the President of the USSR on behalf of the plight of Jews and Christians there. Contact the above address for the closest Embassy branch in your area.

The National Inter-religious Task Force on Soviet Jewry,
1307 South Wabash Avenue, 221,
Chicago, Illonois 60605,
USA

This organisation was founded in 1972 by Sister Ann Gillen to try to bring to both Jewish and Christian communities the message of the common suffering of both Jews and Christians in Eastern Europe and the Soviet Union.

Christian Help For Prisoners of Conscience.
"Let My People Go",
Postbus 80,
1619 ZH Andijk,
Netherlands

A Dutch organisation that regularly sends in letters to the leadership of the Soviet Union, pointing out from scriptural grounds the fact that it is in the Soviet's own best interests to let the Jews go.

"Let My People Go"
Gustav and Elsa Scheller,
44a East Avenue,
Bournemouth, England

Swiss-born business executive Gustav Scheller has taken on the responsibility to help fight for freedom of Soviet Jews. He has organised large rallies on this theme. He and his core group have helped generously in the production of "Gates Of Brass".

Christian Action for Israel
Mr. Claude Duvernoy, International Founder,
111 Uziel Street,
Jerusalem, Israel

Christian Action for Israel,
Mr. Basil Jacobs,
PO Box 11392,
Vlaeberg, Capetown, 8010,
Republic of South Africa

Jerusalem Vistas & International Vistas
Jay and Meridel Rawlings, Directors and Founders,
Box 8232,
Jerusalem 91081, Israel

Keston College,
Rev. Michael Bourdeaux, Director and Founder,
Heathfield Road,
Keston, Kent, BRL 6BA,
England

Keston College is a research institute founded for the study of religion in communist countries and is well respected internationally.

NON-SECTARIAN GROUPS

Committee of 15. (Comite des Quinze),
c/o Julie Davis,
745 Avenue du General Le Clerc,
Boulogne, France

Quasi-Governmental but privately funded.

International Parliamentary Group,
Founded by Senator Charles Grassley and Senator Dennis Deconcini,
The United States Senate,
Washington DC 20510, USA

Purpose: IPG is organised to better co-ordinate unified advocacy of human rights issues in relations with the USSR. By bringing together parliamentarians from the USA, Western Europe, Canada, Israel, and other countries, IPG hopes to raise public awareness of these issues and to promote a united Western approach in bilateral and multilateral relations with the Soviet Union.

Focus: The IPG will focus in three major issues in Soviet human rights performance:

1) National repatriation, freedom of emigration and family reunification as defined by the Helsinki Accords and the Universal Declaration on Human Rights;

2) Religious persecution;

3) The free flow of information and human contacts between the West and the USSR.

INDEPENDENT ORGANISATIONS

Amnesty International,
1 Easton Street,
London WC1 8DJ,
England

Amnesty International is a worldwide movement which is independent of any government political faction, idealogy, economic interest or religious creed. It plays a specific role within the overall spectrum of human rights work.

Cambridge For Soviet Jewry,
Trinity Hall,
Cambridge University,
Cambridge, United Kingdom

Academic Committee on Soviet Jewry,
823 United Nations Plaza,
New York, New York 10019, USA

Amnesty International,
304 West 58th Street,
New York, New York 10019, USA

Commission on Security and Co-operation in Europe,
3257 House Office Building, Annex 2,
Washington DC 20515, USA

Committee of Concerned Scientists,
9 East 40th Street,
New York, New York 10016, USA

Freedom House,
20 West 40th Street,
New York, New York 10018, USA

Helsinki Watch Committee,
205 East 42nd Street,
New York, New York 10017, USA

Religion in Communist Dominated Areas,
475 Riverside Drive,
New York, New York 10027, USA

Dutch Solidarity Committee with Soviet Jewry,
Professor Hevdeikur Beekhof,
Vliarvlindee 7
Leyde, Pays-Bas,
The Netherlands

Congressional Wives for Soviet Jewry,
c/o United States Senate,
Washington DC 20510, USA
Co-chairman – Helen Jackson (widow of Henry Jackson)

These are only a few of the many organisations that exist to help Soviet Jews. Please send us information on other groups with similar aims from around the world and we will publish them in the future.

Conclusion

This book is about one family's attempts to help Russian Jews who want to go to Israel and are prevented by the Soviet system. What can one family do in the face of the largest nation in the world with staggering military might? In the natural it is a foolish struggle. However, as David Ben Gurion once said, "Anyone who becomes involved in Israel and the Jews and doesn't believe in miracles is not a realist."

It is clear that the essence of the Bible was summed up by Jesus when he answered the question of a Hebrew scribe in Jerusalem who asked, "Which is the first commandment of all?"

'Jesus answered him, "The first of all the commandments is, Hear O Israel; The Lord our God is one Lord:

And thou shalt love the Lord thy God with all thy heart, and with all thy soul, and with all thy mind, and with all thy strength: this is the first commandment.

And the second is like, namely this, Thou shalt love thy neighbour as thyself. There is none other commandment greater than these."'

Mark 12:29-31

This means that we really are our brother's keeper and whatever evil happens to one person in some remote part of the world does eventually affect us in our comfortable and various social isolations in the free world. Their pain and cry demands a response, either apathy or action. As a family we have decided on action! – Action on behalf of a persecuted minority, the Jews, and particularly the Soviet Jews, for we know that what happens to them will ultimately happen to us if left unattended.

During the filming of "Gates of Brass", director Bruce Allen reminded us of David's confrontation against Goliath. Here was the greatest example of military might in that day coming against Israel, represented by a youth, albeit one who fought in the name of the Lord of Hosts. David picked up five smooth stones from the river bed, obviously carefully chosen. Accurately thrown from his sling, it struck the giant in the forehead, stunned and felled this champion of the heathen world.

At times we have felt alone much like David must have when confronting Goliath. "Gates of Brass" could be likened to a small stone, while the sling is our proposed world distribution program. Here is where **you** come in. You can read this book, see the film, then choose to do nothing. If, however you choose to become vitally involved, your participation will help to 'sling' the voice of Jews in the Soviet Union around the world. Our united action will help to fell this modern giant in the name of the Lord God of Israel.

Bibliography

BOOKS

Arbella, Irving and Troper, Harold. **None Is Too Many**. Toronto: Lester and Orpen Dennys, 1982.

Barron, John. **KGB Today: Hidden Hand**. London: Coronet, Hodder and Stoughton, 1983.

The Bible. King James Version, NIV Version.

Bourdeaux, Michael. **Risen Indeed – Lessons in Faith From the USSR**. London: Darton, Longman and Todd, Keston Book 16, 1983.

Burnett, Ken. **Why Pray For Israel?** Basingstoke: Marshall, Morgan and Scott, 1983.

Cohen, Richard **Let My People Go.** New York: Popular Library Eagle Books, 1971.

Despagne, Pierre. **Guide de la Prophetie Biblique**. Guide to Bible Prophecy. Cosne sur-Loire, Yverdon Switzerland, 1977.

Eckman, Samuel Lester. **Soviet Policy Towards Jews and Israel**. New York: Shengold Publishers Inc., 1974.

Elazar, Daniel and Dortort, Alysa M. **Understanding the Jewish Agency – A Handbook**. Jerusalem: Jerusalem Centre for Public Affairs, 1984.

Eliav, Arie. **Between Hammer And Sickle**. New York: Signet Books, 1969.

Feingold, Henry L. **The Politics of Rescue**. New York: The Holocaust Library, 1970.

Freemantle, Brian. **KGB**. London and Sydney: McDonald and Co., Futura Books, 1984.

Gilbert, Martin. **Jewish History Atlas**. London: Weidenfeld and Nicolson, 1976.

Gilbert, Martin. **The Jews of Russia**, 3rd ed. Jerusalem: Steimetsky and the Jerusalem Post, 1979.

Israel Pocket Library. **Immigration and Settlement**. Jerusalem: Keter Books, 1973.

Josephson, Elmer A. **Israel, God's Key To World Redemption**. Hillsboro: Bible Light Publications, 1974.

Lambert, Lance. **The Uniqueness Of Israel**. Eastbourne: Kingsway Publications, 1980.

Lightle, Steve; Muelhn, Eberhard; and Fortune, Katie. **Exodus II**. Kingswood, Texas: Hunter Books, 1983.

McQuaid, Elwood. **It Is No Dream**. West Collingswood: The Spearhead Press, 1978.

Meacham, S.M. **It Is Still Not Too Late – The Importance of Christian Action on Behalf of Soviet Jewry**. Jerusalem: The International Christian Embassy, Jerusalem, 1983.

Meir, Golda. **My Life**. London: Futura Books, 1975.

Popular Judaica Library. **The Return To Zion**. Jerusalem: Keter Books, 1974.

Prince, Derek. **The Last Word On The Middle East**. Lincoln VA: Chosen Books, 1982.

Pretal, David. ed. **In Search Of Self – The Soviet Jewish Intelligentsia and the Exodus**. Jerusalem: Mt. Scopus Publication, 1982.

Quinn, Carl Underhill. **The People of Israel**. New York, London: Peebles Press, 1977.

Relfe, Mary Stuart. **The New Money System 666.** Montgomery Ministries Inc. 1982

Rositzke, Harry. **The KGB – The Eyes Of Russia**. London: Sedgwick and Jackson,

Schroeter, Leonard. **The Last Exodus**. Jerusalem: Weidenfeld and Nicolson, 1974.

Shcharansky, Avital and Ben-Joseph, Ilana. **Next Year in Jerusalem**. New York: William Morrow and Co., Inc., 1979.

Shifrin, Avraham. **The First Guidebook To The USSR – Prisons and Concentration Camps**. Uhldingen Seewis: Stephanus Verlog, 1980.

Shulman, Abraham. **Coming Home To Zion**. New York: Doubleday, 1979.

Singer, Dr. Jerome E. **The Case Of Yosef Begun – Analysis and Documents**. Tel Aviv: Faculty of Law, Tel Aviv University, Israel, 1979.

Sterling, Claire. **The Terror Network**. New York: Holt Rhinehart and Winston, 1981.

Taylor, Telford. **Courts Of Terror**. New York: Random Books Vintage Press, 1976.

Walvoord, John F. **Israel In Prophecy**. Grand Rapids: Zondervan Publishing Co., 1970.

Wiesel, Elie. **The Jews Of Silence**. New York: Holt Rinehart and Winston, Inc., 1967.

Periodicals and Articles

Aikman, David and Wright, Louisa. "New Hope for China's Jews." **Time** February 11, 1985

Amnesty International. "A Chronicle Of Current Events." **Journal Of The Human Rights Movemcnt In The USSR** No 64 (1984).

Frankel, Jonathan. **The Soviet Regime and Anti-Zionism – An Analysis** Jerusalem: The Soviet and East European Research Centre, The Hebrew University of Jerusalem, Paper 55, (1984).

Keston College. **Religion in Communist Lands**. Keston: Keston College, 1984. Vol. 12, No. 3: Review of "The Jews of Hope", by Martin Gilbert; and "Soviet Psychiatric Abuse – The Shadow Over World Psychiatry", by Michael Reddaway and Signey Blovck.

Shevchenko, Arkady. "Breaking With Moscow" **Time**, February 11, 18, 1985.

The Jerusalem Post – various articles quoted regarding the subject of Soviet Jewry. (See Chapter notes.)

"Zionists Accused of Undermining The Soviet System." **The Soviet Union And The Middle East**, vol. VIII, No 5. Jerusalem: The Soviet and East European Research Center, (1983).

Reports

Amnesty International. **Annual Report 1984** London: (1984)

Amnesty International. **Prisoners Of Conscience In The USSR – Their Treatment and Conditions** London: (1984).

Amipaz, Gitta. "Jews in the Soviet Union" Israel Information Briefing Report. Jerusalem: Israel Information Center, (1977).

Fain, Benjamin and Verbit, Mervin R. "Jewishness in the Soviet Union." **Report of an Empirical Survey**. Jerusalem: Jerusalem Center for Public Affairs, (1984).

Nurdock, May. "About Israel – Do You Know That?" **Israel Information Briefing Report On "Jews in the Soviet Union"** Jerusalem: (1977).

"The People." **Israel Information Center Report**. Jerusalem: (1979).

Other Sources

1. Notes of Special Seminars, Lectures and Conventions on Soviet Jewry in Jerusalem, 1982, 1983, 1984.

2. Rawlings' personal diaries on various trips to the Soviet Union in 1972, 1983, March and April and 1983, October and November, including personal interviews with Soviet Jews in Moscow, Leningrad and Kiev.

3. Film Interviews – by Jay and Meridel Rawlings for film "Gates of Brass".
— Inside Moscow and Leningrad, October and November, 1983.
— Israel – Jerusalem, Tel Aviv, Arad, Beersheva, November, 1984.
— England – London, December, 1984.

INTERNATIONAL VISTAS

Headquarters – Israel
Box 8232, Jerusalem 91081
Tel. (02) 246027
Telex 26144 BXJMIL ext. 7276

Great Britain
c/o New Wine Press
PO Box 17
Chichester, W Sussex

European Donations
Account No. 162008
Stadtsparkasse Frankfurt/Main, Germany
BLZ 50050102

USA
Box 24630
Dallas, Texas 75224
Tel. (214) 9483411

Canada
243 Broadway
Orangeville, Ontario L9W 1K6
Tel. (519) 9414310

South Africa
PO Box 2212
Honeydew
2040 Johannesburg,
Rep. of S. Africa

Please find enclosed my prepaid order.

BOOKS (postage & handling add $1.00 per book)

☐ "FISHERS AND HUNTERS". Visits to Jewish communities around the world encouraging them to return to Zion. *Large format edition US$6.95 Abridged edition US$3.95*

☐ "GATES OF BRASS". On the plight of Soviet Jews including secret material smuggled out of Russia. The 'behind the scenes' story to the film production by the same title. *US$5.95*

CASSETTE MESSAGES

☐ "WE WILL NOT BE SILENT" *US$3.00*

☐ "REPORT ON TRIP INTO USSR" *US$3.00*

FILMS & VIDEOS (postage & handling add $2.00)

☐ "APPLES OF GOLD" Modern History of Israel (78 min.)

Film		US$995
½" Video	☐ VHS	US$85
	☐ BETA	US$85

☐ "GATES OF BRASS" Plight of Soviet Jews, "Let My People Go"
Film Project. (54 min.)

½" Video	☐ VHS	US$75
	☐ BETA	US$75

☐ "LEBANON AND THE MIDDLE EAST – THE UNTOLD STORY (28 min.)

½" Video	☐ VHS	US$55
	☐ BETA	US$55

☐ Message on Plight of Soviet Jews – "Refuseniks" with exclusive film interviews from the USSR. 45 min.

½" Video	☐ VHS	US$35
	☐ BETA	US$35

Amount enclosed:

Name

Address